The

RAGGED MOUNTAIN PORTABLE WILDERNESS PORTABLE WILDERNESS

ANTHOLOGY

The
RAGGED MOUNTAIN PORTABLE WILDERNESS
ANTHOLOGY

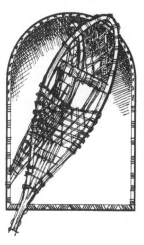

ILLUSTRATIONS BY JAN ADKINS
DESIGN BY BRIAN JONES

RAGGED MOUNTAIN PRESS—CAMDEN, MAINE

Published by Ragged Mountain Press, an imprint of TAB Books.
TAB Books is a division of McGraw-Hill, Inc.

10 9 8 7 6 5 4 3 2 1

Library of Congress Cataloging-in-Publication Data

The Ragged Mountain Portable wilderness anthology / edited by
Jan Adkins.
  p. cm
  Includes bibliographical references (p.) and index.
  ISBN 0-87742-370-9 (acid-free)
  1. Wilderness areas—Quotations, maxims, etc. I. Adkins, Jan.
  PN6084.W47R34 1993   93-8397
  508—dc20   CIP

Questions regarding the content of this book should be
addressed to:
Ragged Mountain Press
P.O. Box 220
Camden, ME 04843

Questions regarding the ordering of this book should be
addressed to:
TAB Books/Ragged Mountain Press
A Division of McGraw-Hill, Inc.
Blue Ridge Summit, PA 17294
1-800-233-1128

A portion of the profits from the sale of each Ragged Mountain
Press book is donated to an environmental cause.

⊛ *The Ragged Mountain Portable Wilderness Anthology* is
   printed on 60-pound Glatfelter Supple, an acid-free paper
that contains 50 percent recycled waste paper (preconsumer) and
10 percent postconsumer waste paper.

Printed by R.R. Donnelley, Crawfordsville, IN.
Production by Molly Mulhern.

copyright page is continued on page 138

CONTENTS

SETTING OUT

THE DARK WIND

Tony Hillerman

Tony Hillerman has written many mystery novels set on the Navajo reservation in Arizona.

He slammed the door behind him and stood facing the glow on the eastern horizon. He yawned and stretched and inhaled deeply of the cold early air. He felt absolutely fine. This was *hozro*. This was the beauty that Changing Woman taught them to attain. This was the feeling of harmony, of being in tune. The orange glow in the east turned to a hot yellow as Chee sang his dawn chant. There was no one in miles to hear him. He shouted it, greeting Dawn Boy, greeting the sun, blessing the new day. "Let beauty walk before me," Chee sang. "Let beauty walk behind me. Let beauty walk all around me." He opened his shirt, extracted his medicine pouch, took out a pinch of pollen, and offered it to the moving air. "In beauty it is finished," Chee sang.

❧❧❧

Afoot and light-hearted I take to the open road,
Healthy, free, the world before me,
The long brown path before me leading wherever
　　I choose.

Henceforth I ask not good fortune, I myself am
　　good fortune,
Henceforth I whimper no more, postpone no more,
　　need nothing,
Done with indoor complaints, libraries, querulous
　　criticisms,
Strong and content, I travel the open road.

　　　　　　　　　　　—from "Song of the Open Road"
　　　　　　　　　　　　　Walt Whitman (1819–1892)

❧❧❧

From

NORTHERN NURSE

Elliott Merrick

*Elliott Merrick wrote eloquently of
life in the far north. In* Northern
Nurse, *he chronicled (in the first person) his wife's two and a half years
as a nurse in Labrador earlier this
century.*

Sound as the logs around me I slept, waking only once to stretch and ache gratefully in the warm, sweet darkness. Johnnie, whose business is travelling, had a quick breakfast of bread and tea into me, our gear collected, the komatik loaded, the dogs harnessed, almost before I could get my eyes open. Long before sunrise we were out on the lake. The wind had dropped utterly, stars were out, the lake a deep blue, the cold like a knife. The blow had hardened the lake and fluted it in pointed patterns which streamed for thirty-five miles between the great bold headlands, now touched with gold. As we flew along, both riding, the shadows of the hills retreated like purple pools that shrink in droughts, and then the sun was up, gleaming on a plain of gold and silver crystals. In the magic of the sunrise I wondered, not that I was there, but that I had never been there before to see it. Where had I been all my life, and what could I have been busy about? . . . .

As the sun rose higher, it tempered the frost, the sledge runners didn't squeak so much, and the team picked up speed. After Green Island had been left behind, our noses didn't hurt when we stuck them out into the breeze. Jim slowed the dogs so we could have a run on the crunching snow. I trotted behind, and it didn't matter about me, how slow I ran, or whether I fell. But Jim ran beside the forward end of the komatik where he could hop on at a moment's notice if the dogs began a spurt as they often do when they smell a seal hole. They will leave a fellow, like as not, if they get a chance, and Heaven knows where they'll go, wrecking the sledge and scattering the gear and ruining their harness on the way.

We hopped on again, tingling and excited, and all of a sudden a great joy flooded me. It had been impossible to start, it was so cold and grim and miserable. But here we were, miles from home already in the sunshine. Already the hills of home were blue behind us, the sun warm, the dogs galloping, the komatik surging. The daily miracle had engulfed us again and I was ashamed that only an hour ago existence had been a burden and oblivion in my bed the only joy.

❧❧❧

In the beginning God gave to every people a cup of clay, and from this cup they drank their life.

—*Northern Paiute proverb*

❧❧❧

From

WALKING THE YUKON

Chris Townsend

Chris Townsend is a contemporary adventurer and veteran of many long hikes, including the 1,000-mile walk chronicled in Walking the Yukon: A Solo Trek Through the Land of Beyond.

I would, as always, be going alone. I know well the arguments that solo hiking in a remote wilderness is foolhardy, dangerous, even irresponsible, but I know even more the great rewards that await the lone wanderer, rewards that can only be glimpsed by those who walk in groups. Alone I would be able to open myself up to the wilderness, to ready all my senses for what was offered, to learn what the mountains and forests, the rivers and lakes had to teach me. I was not going in order to observe the land from the outside, to view it as a series of picture postcards, but rather to become part of it, to feel that harmony with the natural world that comes only after days alone. This was the real purpose of the walk, and the linking of two points on the map merely an excuse to satisfy rational requirements and goad me onward each day. Perhaps one day I'll head out into the wilderness and just sit under a tree for a summer, but for now I need a goal, however distant and hazy.

Walking is the best way to gain understanding of a place, to assimilate its rhythms and time scales. All landscapes are dynamic, whether the movement is the infinitesimally slow erosion of a cliff or the swift thunder of an avalanche ripping trees from a hillside. Water and sky move constantly. Life is an essential part of any landscape too—the growth and decay of plants, the flights of birds, migrations of animals. To sit still is to watch the land flow past, to walk is to move with it. Mechanized travel leaves the land behind, disconnecting us from it. One of the problems of modern times is that we are separated from the world that supports us by the speed with which we traverse it. Walking is the best way to know a place, perhaps the only way.

❧❧❧❧

In soloing—as in other activities—it is far easier to start something than it is to finish it.

—20 Hours: 40 Minutes—Our Flight in Friendship
Amelia Earhart (1897–1937)

❧❧❧❧

Two roads diverged in a yellow wood,
And sorry I could not travel both
And be one traveler, long I stood
And looked down one as far as I could
To where it bent in the undergrowth;

Then took the other, as just as fair,
And having perhaps the better claim,
Because it was grassy and wanted wear;
Though as for that, the passing there
Had worn them really about the same,

And both that morning equally lay
In leaves no step had trodden black.
Oh, I kept the first for another day!
Yet knowing how way leads on to way,
I doubted if I should ever come back.

I shall be telling this with a sigh
Somewhere ages and ages hence:
Two roads diverged in a wood, and I—
I took the one less traveled by,
And that has made all the difference.

—"The Road Not Taken"
Robert Frost (1874–1963)

From

LETTERS OF A WOMAN HOMESTEADER

Elinore Pruitt Stewart

Elinore Pruitt, a widow, and her young daughter Jerrine headed West at the turn of the century to carve out a new life. Pruitt wrote letters to a friend in the East about her efforts to claim and "prove" her land, and her eventual marriage to Mr. Stewart, for whom she kept house. These letters were first published in The Atlantic Monthly *in 1913.*

The sun was just gilding the hilltops when we arose. Everything, even the barrenness, was beautiful. We have had frosts, and the quaking aspens were a trembling field of gold as far up the stream as we could see. We were 'way up above them and could look far across the valley. We could see the silvery gold of the willows, the russet and bronze of the currants, and patches of cheerful green showed where the pines were. The splendor was relieved by a background of sober gray-green hills, but even on them gay streaks and patches of yellow showed where rabbitbrush grew. We washed our faces at the spring,—the grasses that grew around the edge and dipped into the water were loaded with ice,—our rabbit was done to a turn, so I made some delicious coffee, Jerrine got herself a can of water, and we breakfasted. Shortly afterwards we started again. We didn't know where we were going, but we were on our way.

My vicinity affords many good walks; and though for so many years I have walked almost every day, and sometimes for several days together, I have not yet exhausted them. An absolutely new prospect is a great happiness, and I can still get this any afternoon. Two or three hours' walking will carry me to as strange a country as I ever expect to see.

—*from "Walking"*
Henry David Thoreau (1817–1862)

❦❦❦

From

IN DEFENSE OF NATURE

John Hay

John Hay is a nature writer and poet whose works include The Run, The Atlantic Shore, The Great Beach, Nature's Year, *and* In Defense of Nature.

Contemporary travel has a curiously anesthetizing, self-enclosed quality. You can go several hundred miles in the wrong direction, as I once did to my embarrassment, and if you get the next flight back, not lose more than a couple of hours. The fantastic but hardly noticed speed, the dark-suited passengers reading the stock market quotations as if they were not flying over the edge of a great sea or complex landscape at all but were in a city bus—even the possibility of an unregarded death, makes travel not so much a matter of bypassing time and distance as losing track of transitions. We take our cities with us and join them together as we go. It amounts to a new kind of insularity. Speed past sound, forced immediacy, puts all the world in the same room.

❦❦❦

From

WINTER SUNSHINE

John Burroughs

John Burroughs (1837–1921) was an American naturalist and writer. This selection is from his essay, "The Exhilaration of the Road," from Winter Sunshine *published in 1875.*

When I see the discomforts that able-bodied American men will put up with rather than go a mile or half a mile on foot, the abuses they will tolerate and encourage, crowding the streetcar on a little fall in the temperature or the appearance of an inch or two of snow, packing up to overflowing, dangling to the straps, treading on each other's toes, breathing each other's breaths, crushing the women and children, hanging by tooth and nail to a square inch of the platform, imperiling their limbs and killing the horses—I think the commonest tramp in the street has good reason to felicitate himself on his rare privilege of going afoot. Indeed, a race that neglects or despises this primitive gift, that fears the touch of the soil, that has no footpaths, no community of ownership in the land which they imply, that warns off the walker as a trespasser, that knows no way but the highway, the carriage way, that forgets the stile, the footbridge, that even ignores the rights of the pedestrian in the public road, providing no escape for him but in the ditch or up the bank, is in a fair way to far more serious degeneracy.

❧❧❧

In Endymion, I leaped headlong into the sea, and thereby have become better acquainted with the soundings, the quicksands, and the rocks, than if I had

stayed upon the green shore, and piped a silly pipe,
and took tea and comfortable advice.

—*from* Letters
John Keats (1795–1821)

❧❧❧❧

From

HISTORIC WATERWAYS
SIX HUNDRED MILES OF CANOEING DOWN THE ROCK, FOX, AND WISCONSIN RIVERS

Reuben Gold Thwaites

*Reuben Gold Thwaites (1853–1913)
was an American historian who
wrote about early explorations of the
upper Midwest and the West.*

There is a generally accepted notion that a brief
summer vacation, if at all obtainable in this busy
life of ours, must be spent in a flight as far afield as
time will allow; that the popular resorts in the mountains, by the seaside, or on the margins of the upper
lakes must be sought for rest and enjoyment; that
neighborhood surroundings should, in the mad rush
for change of air and scene, be left behind. The result
is that your average vacationist—if I may be allowed
to coin a needed word—knows less of his own state
than of any other, and is inattentive to the delights of
nature which await inspection within the limits of his
own horizon.

But let him mount his bicycle, his saddle horse, or
his family carriage, and start out upon a gypsy tour of
a week or two along the country roads, exploring the
hills and plains and valleys of—say his congressional
district; or, better by far, take his canoe, and with his

best friend for a messmate explore the nearest river from source to mouth, and my word for it he will find novelty and fresh air enough to satisfy his utmost cravings; and when he comes to return to his counter, his desk, or his study, he will be conscious of having discovered charms in his own locality which he has in vain sought in the accustomed paths of the tourist.

❦❦❦

From

MY FIRST SUMMER IN THE SIERRA

John Muir

John Muir (1838–1914), a Scottish-born naturalist and writer, concentrated his studies on Yosemite Valley from 1868–1874. The year was 1869, the same year that John Wesley Powell explored the Colorado River.

June 13. Another glorious Sierra day in which one seems to be dissolved and absorbed and sent pulsing onward we know not where. Life seems neither long nor short, and we take no more heed to save time or make haste than do the trees and stars. This is true freedom, a good practical sort of immortality. . . .

July 15. Followed the Mono Trail up the eastern rim of the basin nearly to its summit, then turned off southward to a small shallow valley that extends to the edge of the Yosemite, which we reached about noon, and encamped. After luncheon I made haste to high ground, and from the top of the ridge on the west side of Indian Cañon gained the noblest view of the summit peaks I have ever yet enjoyed. Nearly all the upper basin of the Merced was displayed, with its sublime domes and cañons, dark up-sweeping forests, and glorious array of white peaks deep in the sky, every feature glowing, radiating beauty that pours into our flesh and bones like heat rays from fire. Sunshine over all; no breath of wind to stir the brooding calm. Never before had I seen so glorious a landscape, so boundless an affluence of sublime mountain beauty. The most extravagant description I might give of this view to anyone who has not seen similar landscapes with his own eyes would not so much as hint its grandeur and the spiritual glow that covered it. I shouted and gesticulated in a wild burst of ecstasy, much to the astonishment of St. Bernard Carlo, who came running up to me, manifesting in his intelligent eyes a puzzled concern that was very ludicrous, which had the effect of bringing me to my senses. A brown bear, too, it would seem, had been a spectator of the show I had made of myself, for I had gone but a few yards when I started one from a thicket of brush. He evidently considered me dangerous, for he ran away very fast, tumbling over the tops of the tangled manzanita bushes in his haste. Carlo drew back, with his ears depressed as if afraid, and kept looking me in the face, as if expecting me to pursue and shoot, for he had seen many a bear battle in his day.

Following the ridge, which made a gradual descent to the south, I came at length to the brow of that massive cliff that stands between Indian Cañon and Yosemite Falls, and here the far-famed valley came suddenly into view throughout almost its whole extent. The noble walls—sculptured into endless variety of domes and gables, spires and battlements and plain mural precipices—all a-tremble with the thunder tones of the falling water. The level bottom seemed to be dressed like a garden—sunny meadows here and there, and groves of pine and oak; the river of Merced sweeping in majesty through the midst of them and flashing back the sunbeams. The great Tissiack, or Half-Dome, rising at the upper end of the valley to a height of nearly a mile, is nobly proportioned and life-like, the most impressive of all the rocks, holding the eye in devout admiration, calling it back again and again from falls or meadows, or even the mountains beyond,—marvelous cliffs, marvelous in sheer dizzy depth and sculpture, types of endurance. Thousands of years have they stood in the sky exposed to rain, snow, frost, earthquake and avalanche, yet they still wear the bloom of youth.

I rambled along the valley rim to the westward; most of it is rounded off on the very brink, so that it is not easy to find places where one may look clear down the face of the wall to the bottom. When such places were found, and I had cautiously set my feet and drawn my body erect, I could not help fearing a little that the rock might split off and let me down, and what a down!—more than three thousand feet. Still my limbs did not tremble, nor did I feel the least uncertainty as to the reliance to be placed on them. My only fear was that a flake on the granite, which in some places showed joints more or less open and run-ning parallel with the face of the cliff, might give way. After withdrawing from such places, excited with the view I had got, I would say to myself, "Now don't go out on the verge again." But in the face of Yosemite scenery cautious remonstrance is vain; under its spell one's body seems to go where it likes and with a will over which we seem to have scarce any control.

After a mile or so of this memorable cliff work I approached Yosemite Creek, admiring its easy, grace-ful, confident gestures as it comes bravely forward in its narrow channel, singing the last of its mountain songs on its way to its fate—a few rods more over the shining granite, then down half a mile in showy foam to another world, to be lost in the Merced, where climate, vegetation, inhabitants, all are different. Emerging from its last gorge, it glides in wide lace-like rapids down a smooth incline into a pool where it seems to rest and compose its gray, agitated waters before taking the grand plunge, then slowly slipping over the lip of the pool basin, it descends another glossy slope with rapidly accelerated speed to the brink of the tremendous cliff, and with sublime, fateful confidence springs out free in the air.

I took off my shoes and stockings and worked my way cautiously down alongside the rushing flood, keeping my feet and hands pressed firmly on the polished rock. The booming, roaring water, rushing past close to my head, was very exciting. I had expected that the sloping apron would terminate with the perpendicular wall of the valley, and that from the foot of it, where it is less steeply inclined, I should be able to lean far enough out to see the forms and behavior of the fall all the way down to the bottom. But I found that there was yet another small brow over which I could not see, and which appeared to be too steep for mortal feet. Scanning it keenly, I discovered a narrow shelf about three inches wide on the very brink, just wide enough for a rest for one's heels. But there seemed to be no way of reaching it over so steep a brow. At length, after careful scrutiny of the surface, I found an irregular edge of a flake of the rock some distance back from the margin of the torrent. If I was to get down to the brink at all that rough edge, which might offer slight finger-holds, was the only way. But the slope beside it looked dangerously smooth and steep, and the swift roaring flood beneath, overhead, and beside me was very nerve-trying. I therefore concluded not to venture farther, but did nevertheless. Tufts of artemisia were growing in clefts of the rock near by, and I filled my mouth with the bitter leaves, hoping they might help to prevent giddiness. Then, with a caution not known in ordinary circumstances, I crept down safely to the little ledge, got my heels well planted on it, then shuffled in a horizontal direction twenty or thirty feet until close to the outplunging current, which, by the time it had descended thus far, was already white. Here I obtained a perfectly free view down into the heart of the snowy, changing throng of comet-like streamers, into which the body of the fall soon separates.

While perched on that narrow niche I was not distinctly conscious of danger. The tremendous grandeur of the fall in form and sound and motion, acting at close range, smothered the sense of fear, and in such places one's body takes keen care for safety on its own account. How long I remained down there, or how I returned, I can hardly tell. Anyhow I had a glorious time, and got back to camp about dark, enjoying triumphant exhilaration soon followed by dull weariness. Hereafter I'll try to keep from such extravagant, nerve-straining places. Yet such a day is well worth venturing for. My first view of the High Sierra, first view looking down into Yosemite, the death song of Yosemite Creek, and its flight over the vast cliff, each one of these is of itself enough for a great life-long landscape fortune—a most memorable day of days—enjoyment enough to kill if that were possible.

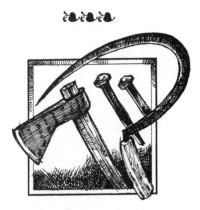

A WOMAN TENDERFOOT

Grace Seton-Thompson

*Grace Seton-Thompson (1872–1959)
was an American writer, poet, feminist, and lecturer.*

I know what it means to be a miner and a cowboy, and have risked my life when need be, *but*, best of all, I have felt the charm of the glorious freedom, the quick rushing blood, the bounding motion, of the wild life, the joy of the living and of the doing, of the mountain and the plain; I have learned to know and feel some, at least, of the secrets of the Wild Ones.

THE WINTER BEACH

Charlton Ogburn, Jr.

The Winter Beach is Charlton Ogburn's account of a trip from Mount Desert Island in Maine to the Outer Banks in North Carolina.

You find also that traveling alone compares with traveling in company as voyaging under sail compares with voyaging by steamship. Bringing a lesser measure of circumstance with you, you are more the creature of circumstances around you. You miss much that an observant and reflective partner would point out but at the same time you are more possessed by the sensations the scene around you induces. You may sometimes at night (to be honest) feel yourself a deserted and lightless house through which the gusts of wind blow dolefully, but that is simply the price you pay for being more receptive to the atmosphere around you—in every way.

OUTDOOR LIFE

THE MAINE WOODS

Henry David Thoreau

Henry David Thoreau (1817–1862) visited Maine in 1846, 1853, and 1857. His journals from these trips were published as The Maine Woods *two years after his death.*

The following will be a good outfit for one who wishes to make an excursion of *twelve* days into the Maine woods in July, with a companion, and one Indian for the same purposes that I did.

Wear—a check shirt, stout old shoes, thick socks, a neck ribbon, thick waistcoat, thick pants, old Kossuth hat, a linen sack.

Carry—in an India-rubber knapsack, with a large flap, two shirts (check), one pair thick socks, one pair drawers, one flannel shirt, two pocket-handkerchiefs, a light India-rubber coat or a thick woollen one, two bosoms and collars to go and come with, one napkin, pins, needles, thread, one blanket, best gray, seven feet long.

Tent—six by seven feet, and four feet high in middle, will do; veil and gloves and insect-wash, or, better, mosquito-bars to cover all night; best pocket-map, and perhaps description of the route; compass; plant-book and red blotting-paper; paper and stamps, botany, small pocket spy-glass for birds, pocket microscope, tape-measure, insect-boxes.

Axe, full size if possible, jackknife, fish-lines, two only apiece, with a few hooks and corks ready, and with pork for bait in a packet, rigged; matches (some also in a small vial in the waistcoat pocket); soap, two pieces; large knife and iron spoon (for all); three or four old newspapers, much twine, and several rags for dish-cloths; twenty feet of strong cord, four-quart tin pail for kettle, two tin dippers, three tin plates, a fry-pan.

Provisions—Soft hardbread, twenty-eight pounds; pork, sixteen pounds; sugar, twelve pounds; one pound black tea or three pounds coffee, one box of a pint of salt, one quart Indian meal, to fry fish in; six lemons, good to correct the pork and warm water; perhaps two or three pounds of rice, for variety. You will probably get some berries, fish, etc., beside.

A gun is not worth the carriage, unless you go as hunters. The pork should be in an open keg, sawed to fit; the sugar, tea or coffee, meal, salt, etc., should be put in separate water-tight India-rubber bags, which have been proved to be water-tight and durable. Expense of preceding outfit is twenty-four dollars.

❧❧❧❧❧

LETTERS OF A WOMAN HOMESTEADER

Elinore Pruitt Stewart

After driving all day over what seemed a level desert of sand, we came about sundown to a beautiful cañon, down which we had to drive for a couple of miles before we could cross. In the cañon the shadows had already fallen, but when we looked up we could see the last shafts of sunlight on the tops of the great bare buttes. Suddenly a great wolf started from somewhere and galloped along the edge of the cañon, outlined black and clear by the setting sun. His curiosity overcame him at last, so he sat down and waited to see what manner of beast we were. I reckon he was disappointed for he howled most dismally. I thought of Jack London's "The Wolf."

After we quitted the cañon I saw the most beautiful sight. It seemed as if we were driving through a golden haze. The violet shadows were creeping up between the hills, while away back of us the snow-capped peaks were catching the sun's last rays. On every side of us stretched the poor, hopeless desert, the sage, grim and determined to live in spite of starvation, and the great, bare, desolate buttes. The beautiful colors turned to amber and rose, and then to the general tone, dull gray. Then we stopped to camp, and such a scurrying around to gather brush for the fire and to get supper! Everything tasted so good! Jerrine ate like a man. Then we raised the wagon tongue and spread the wagon sheet over it and made a bedroom for us women. We made our beds on the warm, soft sand and went to bed.

It was too beautiful a night to sleep, so I put my head out to look and to think. I saw the moon come up and hang for a while over the mountain as if it were discouraged with the prospect, and the big white stars flirted shamelessly with the hills. I saw a coyote come trotting along and I felt sorry for him, having to hunt food in so barren a place, but when presently I heard the whirr of wings I felt sorry for the sage chickens he had disturbed.

From

A WOMAN'S JOURNEY ON THE APPALACHIAN TRAIL

Cindy Ross

Cindy Ross gained many insights as she hiked the 2,100-mile Appalachian Trail.

One learns to make-do.
One learns to make the best of very little.

I use sticks to hold my bun together, large smooth leaves for toilet paper, baking soda for deodorant and tooth paste; and glowing candlelight in place of electricity.

I actually SEW my underwear . . . mend the elastic, patch my pants, darn my socks. Nothing is thrown away. Even when my clothes literally fall off me, I recycle it and use it as rags. My washing machine is a stream and my dryer is the sun, as my clothes hang on the back of my pack.

I can learn to make-do and do without nearly everything, except people. People who care and love me. People I can hug.

From

THREE MEN IN A BOAT

Jerome K. Jerome

Jerome K. Jerome wrote Three Men in a Boat, *his classic account of rowing up the Thames River, in 1889.*

Camping out in rainy weather is not pleasant. It is evening. You are wet through, and there is a good two inches of water in the boat, and all the things are damp. You find a place on the banks that is not quite so puddly as other places you have seen, and you land and lug out the tent, and two of you proceed to fix it.

It is soaked and heavy, and it flops around, and tumbles down on you, and clings round your head and makes you mad. The rain is pouring steadily down all the time. It is difficult enough to fix a tent in dry weather; in wet, the task becomes herculean. Instead of helping you, it seems to you that the other man is simply playing the fool. Just as you get your side beautifully fixed, he gives it a hoist from his end, and spoils it all.

"Here! What are *you* up to?" you call out.

"What are you up to?" he retorts. "Leggo, can't you?"

"Don't pull it; you've got it all wrong, you stupid ass!" you shout.

"No, I haven't," he yells back; "let go your side!"

"I tell you you've got it all wrong!" you roar, wishing that you could get at him; and you give your ropes a lug that pulls all his pegs out.

"Ah, the bally idiot!" you hear him mutter to himself; and then comes a savage haul, and away goes your side. You lay down the mallet and start to go round and tell him what you think about the whole business, and, at the same time, he starts round in the same direction to come and explain his views to you. And you follow each other round and round, swearing at one another, until the tent tumbles down in a heap, and leaves you looking at each other across its ruins, then you both indignantly exclaim, in the same breath:

"There you are! What did I tell you?"

Meanwhile the third man, who has been bailing out the boat, and who has spilled the water down his sleeve, and has been cursing away to himself steadily for the last ten minutes, wants to know what the thundering blazes you're playing at, and why the blarmed tent isn't up yet.

At last, somehow or other, it does get up, and you land the things. It is hopeless attempting to make a wood fire so you light the methylated spirit stove, and crowd round that.

Rainwater is the chief article of diet at supper. The bread is two-thirds rainwater, the beefsteak-pie is exceedingly rich in it, and the jam, and the butter, and the salt, and the coffee have all combined with it to make soup.

From

WOODCRAFT

N e s s m u k

George W. Sears, using the pen name Nessmuk, encouraged thousands of people to take to the woods and "rough it." His book, Woodcraft, *was first published in 1920 and is still in print today.*

With a large majority of prospective tourists and outers, "camping out" is a leading factor in the summer vacation. And during the long winter months they are prone to collect in little knots and talk much of camps, fishing, hunting, and "roughing it." The last phrase is very popular and always cropping out in the talks on matters pertaining to a vacation in the woods. I dislike the phrase. We do not go to the green woods and crystal waters to rough it, we go to smooth it. We get it rough enough at home; in towns and cities; in shops, offices, stores, banks—anywhere that we may be placed—with the necessity always present of being on time and up to our work; of providing for the dependent ones; of keeping up, catching up, or getting left. "Alas for the life-long battle, whose bravest slogan is bread."

෧ඎ෧ඎ෧ඎ

From

THE COMPLETE WILDERNESS PADDLER

James West Davidson and John Rugge

> *James West Davidson and John Rugge used their trip on the Moisie River in Quebec as a jumping-off point for* The Complete Wilderness Paddler, *their best-selling guide to wilderness whitewater canoeing.*

We turned to Science to solve the problem of bugs, and discovered we should have known better. Think about it. Science is still looking for ways to cure cancer, leukemia, and muscular dystrophy; all of the money for lasers, electron microscopes, and other sophisticated equipment gets funneled into these areas. The mosquito researchers get a few leftover Bunsen burners and some out-of-date Venus's-flytraps.

And to be frank, who can blame the big charity drives for taking their money elsewhere? How generous would *you* be with some lady soliciting for the Mosquito March of Dimes?

❧❧❧

From

DANGEROUS RIVER

R. M. Patterson

R. M. Patterson and his friend, Gordon Matthews, spent a year prospecting and trapping along the South Nahanni River in Canada's Northwest Territories in the 1920s. Dangerous River is about that experience.

This was the day of the new hatch of mosquitoes, and several thousand of these keen young sapsuckers were actively on the job, experimenting with human blood and evidently enjoying it. The big, old mosquitoes that Nature so wrong-headedly nurses through the winter to prevent the extinction of the race are deliberate even to the point of fussiness. One can deal with them as they stroll about on the back of the hand, searching for some dainty titbit. But the illimitable hordes of June are in a hurry: they land with all the fury of youth, and where they land they drill, in a second, through the toughest hide: death means nothing to them—it merely makes room for more. The imminence of rain excites these pests to a frenzy, and on this occasion the daily thunderstorm was working up; above the canyon ranges black clouds were climbing up into the blue with a yellow, angry sunset beneath them—and soon the storm broke with a crash of thunder; flash after flash struck the Twisted Mountain, and I lay inside my net listening contentedly to the maddened hum of the mosquitoes and the roar of the torrential rain.

❧❧❧❧

From

THE TRAVELS OF WILLIAM BARTRAM

William Bartram

William Bartram (1739–1823) was a self-taught American botanist who traveled in the Carolinas, the Alleghenies, the Catskills, and Florida in search of new plants. This passage is from his book, The Travels of William Bartram, *which was first published in Philadelphia in 1791, though the events it describes took place years earlier. The following description is from the St. Johns River, Florida.*

I had now swamps and marshes on both sides of me; and evening coming on apace, I began to look out for high land to encamp on; but the extensive marshes seemed to have no bounds, and it was almost dark when I found a tolerably suitable place, and at last was constrained to take up with a narrow strip of high shelly bank, on the west side. Great numbers of crocodiles were in sight on both shores. I ran my bark on shore at a perpendicular bank four or five feet above the water, just by the roots and under the spreading limbs of a great live oak: this appeared to have been an ancient camping place by Indians and strolling adventurers, from ash heaps and old rotten fire-brands and chunks, scattered about on the surface of the ground; but was now evidently the harbour and landing-place of some sovereign alligator: there led up from it a deep beaten path or road, which was a convenient ascent.

I did not approve of my intended habitation from these circumstances; and no sooner had I landed and moored my canoe to the roots of the tree, than I saw a huge crocodile rising up from the bottom close by me, who, when he perceived that I saw him, plunged down again under my vessel. This determined me to be on my guard, and in time to provide against a troublesome night. I took out of my boat every moveable, which I carried upon the bank; then chose my lodging close to my canoe, under the spreading oak, as hereabouts only, the ground was open and clear of high grass and bushes, and consequently I had some room to stir and look round about. I then proceeded to collect firewood, which I found difficult to procure. Here were standing a few orange trees. As for provisions, I had saved one or two barbecued trout, the remains of my last evening's collection, in tolerable good order, though the sultry heats of the day had injured them; yet by stewing them up afresh with the lively juice of Oranges, they served well enough for my supper, as I had by this time but little relish or appetite for my victuals; for constant watching at night against the attacks of alligators, stinging of musquitoes and sultry heats of the day, together with the fatigues of working my bark, had almost deprived me of every desire but that of ending my troubles as speedily as possible . . . I stretched myself along before my fire; having the river, my little harbour, and the stern of my vessel in view; and now through fatigue and weariness I fell asleep. But this happy temporary release from cares and troubles I enjoyed but a few moments, when I was awakened and greatly surprised, by the terrifying screams of Owls in the deep swamps around me; and what increased my extreme misery was the difficulty of getting quite awake, and yet hearing at the same time such screaming and shouting, which increased and spread every way for miles around, in dreadful peals vibrating through the dark extensive forests, meadows, and lakes. I could not after this surprise recover my former peaceable state and tranquillity of mind and repose, during the long night; and I believe it was happy for me that I was awakened, for at that moment the crocodile was dashing my canoe against the roots of the tree, endeavouring to get into her for the fish, which I however prevented. Another time in the night I believe I narrowly escaped being dragged into the river by him; for when again through excessive fatigue I had fallen asleep, but was again awakened by the screaming owl, I found the monster on the top of the bank, his head towards me, not above two yards distant; when starting up, and seizing my fusee well loaded, which I always kept under my head in the night time, he drew back and plunged into the water. . . . As soon as I discovered the first signs of day-light, I arose, got all my effects and implements on board, and set sail, proceeding upwards, hoping to give the musquitoes the slip, who were now, by the cool morning dews and breezes, driven to their shelter and hiding places. I was mistaken however in these conjectures, for great numbers of them, which had concealed themselves in my boat, as soon as the sun arose, began to revive, and sting me on my legs, which obliged me to land in order to get bushes to beat them out of their quarters.

꙳꙳꙳

From

THE JOURNALS OF LEWIS AND CLARK

Meriwether Lewis and William Clark

Meriwether Lewis (1774–1809) and William Clark (1770–1838) explored the Louisiana Purchase in 1804–1806 under commission from Thomas Jefferson, going up the Missouri to the Continental Divide and descending the Columbia River to the Pacific. This passage was written by Lewis.

June 13, 1805: My fare is really sumptuous this evening; buffaloes humps, tongues and marrowbones, fine trout parched meal pepper and salt, and a good appetite. The last is not considered the least of the luxuries.

July 24, 1805: our trio of pests still invade and obstruct us on all occasions, these are the Musquetoes, eye gnats and prickley pears, equal to any three curses that ever poor Egypt laiboured under, except the *Mahometant yoke.*

M. Lewis

From

WOODCRAFT

Nessmuk

It was published in *Forest and Stream* in the summer of 1880, and again in '83. It has been pretty
widely quoted and adopted, and I have never known it
to fail: Three ounces pine tar, two ounces castor oil,
one ounce pennyroyal oil. Simmer all together over a
slow fire, and bottle for use. You will hardly need more
than a two-ounce vial full in a season. One ounce has
lasted me six weeks in the woods. Rub it in thoroughly
and liberally at first, and after you have established a
good glaze, a little replenishing from day to day will be
sufficient. And don't fool with soap and towels where
insects are plenty. A good safe coat of this varnish
grows better the longer it is kept on—and it is cleanly
and wholesome. If you get your face and hands crocky
or smutty about the camp-fire, wet the corner of your
handkerchief and rub it off, not forgetting to apply the
varnish at once, wherever you have cleaned it off. Last
summer I carried a cake of soap and a towel in my
knapsack through the North Woods for a seven weeks'
tour, and never used either a single time. When I had
established a good glaze on the skin, it was too valuable to be sacrificed for any weak whim connected with
soap and water. When I struck a woodland hotel, I
found soap and towels plenty enough. I found the mix-
ture gave one's face the ruddy tanned look supposed to
be indicative of health and hard muscle. A thorough
ablution in the public wash basin reduced the color,
but left the skin very soft and smooth; in fact, as a
lotion for the skin it is excellent. It is a soothing and
healing application for poisonous bites already
received.

From

THE LURE OF THE LABRADOR WILD

Dillon Wallace

Leonidas Hubbard signed up Dillon Wallace, a friend, and George Elson, a Cree guide, to accompany him on a trip to explore the interior of Labrador in 1903. Wallace wrote The Lure of the Labrador Wild *when he returned to the United States.*

I remember that while we sat by the fire that evening George produced from somewhere in the recesses of his pockets a New York Central Railroad timetable on which was printed a buffet lunch menu, and handed it to us with the suggestion that we give our orders for breakfast. Hubbard examined it and quickly said:

"Give me a glass of cream, some graham gems, marmalade, oatmeal and cream, a jelly omelette, a sirloin steak, lyonnaise potatoes, rolls, and a pot of chocolate. And you might bring me also," he added, "a plate of griddle cakes and maple syrup."

Every dish on that menu card from end to end we thoroughly discussed, our ultimate conclusion being that each of us would take a full portion of everything on the list and might repeat the order.

❧❧❧

Time is but the stream I go a-fishing in.

—*"Where I Lived, and What I Lived For" from* Walden
Henry David Thoreau

❧❧❧

From

IN THE LAND OF THE GRASSHOPPER SONG

Mary Ellicott Arnold and Mabel Reed

Mary Ellicott Arnold and Mabel Reed traveled west to teach school in the Klamath River (California) Indian country in 1908–1909.

The standard practice is to put bacon in cold water, then put it on the stove. When the water comes to a boil, the bacon is considered cooked. It is then a pulpy, gelatinous affair and generally a little rancid. As a finishing touch, you pour the greasy bacon water over the beans and the fried potatoes. Tea and coffee making also have peculiarities. You put a pinch of coffee or tea into your pot. Then you put it on the stove and boil it up. Each day you keep adding more pinches, and boiling them, until the pot is full of grounds. Then you dig out your grounds and start fresh. So far, we have never had the luck to be anywhere when they started fresh. Generally there will be frying-pan bread (soda biscuit) and dried-apple pie. Neither very good. And that is all. At best you eat sparingly, unless driven by hunger.

꙳꙳꙳

Angling may be said to be so like the mathematics, that it can never be fully learnt.

—*from* Compleat Angler
Izaak Walton (1593–1683)

꙳꙳꙳

From

THE JOURNALS OF
LEWIS AND CLARK

Meriwether Lewis and William Clark

*After they reached the Pacific, Lewis
and Clark built Fort Clatsop on the
Columbia River and wintered over
there, hoping to find ships to take
them home. This entry was written
at Fort Clatsop.*

January 29th 1806:   Nothing worthy of notice
occurred today. our fare is the flesh of lean elk
boiled with pure water, and a little salt. the whale
blubber which we have used very sparingly is now
exhausted. on this food I do not feel strong, but enjoy
the most perfect health; a keen appetite supplys in a
great degree the want of more luxurious sauses or
dishes, and still renders my ordinary meals not unin-
teresting to me, for I find myself sometimes enquiring
of the cook whether dinner or breakfast is ready.

From

THE EXPLORATION OF
THE COLORADO RIVER
AND ITS CANYONS

John Wesley Powell

*John Wesley Powell took a crew of
nine men in four boats to explore the
Green and Colorado rivers in 1869,
recording his findings in* The Exploration of the Colorado River and

Its Canyons. *He made this observation near the junction of the Green and Colorado rivers.*

Now we return to camp. While eating supper we very naturally speak of better fare, as musty bread and spoiled bacon are not palatable. Soon I see Hawkins down by the boat, taking up the sextant—rather a strange proceeding for him—and I question him concerning it. He replies that he is trying to find the latitude and longitude of the nearest pie.

❧❧❧❧

From

PETER KALM'S TRAVELS IN NORTH AMERICA
Peter Kalm

Peter Kalm was a Swedish botanist who traveled in the mid-Atlantic region of America for two and a half years, starting in the fall of 1748.

The vast woods and uninhabited grounds between Albany and Canada contain immense swarms of gnats [mosquitoes] which annoy the travellers. To be in some measure secured against these insects some besmear their face with butter or grease, for the gnats do not like to settle on greasy places. The great heat makes boots very uncomfortable; but to prevent the gnats from stinging the legs they wrap some paper round them, under the stockings. Some travellers wear caps which cover the whole face, and some have gauze over their eyes. At night they lie in tents, if they can carry any with them, and make a great fire at the entrance so that smoke will drive them away.

❧❧❧❧

They who have been traveling long on the steppes of Tartary say: "On reëntering cultivated lands, the agitation, perplexity, and turmoil of civilization oppressed and suffocated us; the air seemed to fail us, and we felt every moment as if about to die of asphyxia."

—from "Walking"
Henry David Thoreau

ON THE WATER

From

DANGEROUS RIVER

R. M. Patterson

I knew that it was now or never. I turned the canoe over, strapped my field glass to the seat, laid the pole along the thwarts and put a spare paddle on the floor. Then I lifted the canoe and set it gently in the river, holding it while I laid a big rock in the nose to partly balance my weight in the trail. All was ready, and I coiled the trackline, stepped in and shoved off. There is something beautifully final in certain phases of river travel: you make your decision and pick your course, and after that the rest is all action. You are committed, and there is no turning back—you must make it or swamp. The result is a supreme peak of physical effort and a split-second awareness of changing water: and mentally a sort of cold excitement and exhilaration—a high point of living.

From

"TWO GIRLS IN A CANOE"

Isobel Knowles

Isobel Knowles and her canoeing partner wore long skirts when they paddled the Gatineau in Quebec. This article about the trip was published in Cosmopolitan Magazine *in 1905.*

I am an experienced canoeist, but those rapids on the upper Gatineau caught me unawares. We had been paddling for mile after mile through comparatively sluggish water, when a sudden narrowing of the channel brought us to the head of a gorge down which the river tossed and roared angrily like a living thing.

We were two in the canoe, and we had passed the rapids on our way up the week before, but did not recognize them now that we approached from the opposite direction. Then we had portaged around them, carrying the canoe on our shoulders, over trunks of fallen trees and through the matted branches of the brushwood. Since that time we had seen much of river scenery, seen hills rising beyond hills till lost in the distant haze, great silent forests of spruce and pine, and placid sheets of crystal lake, and now, toward the close of our two weeks' outing, we were two days' travel from the nearest outpost of civilization.

So stealthily had the swiftening water above the turn carried us on, that we were going at a ten-mile-an-hour gait before I realized our position. Then the sudden leap of the canoe, the roll and pitch of the water under us, warned that the time to land had passed. There was no turning back against a ten-mile current, no making for either side, where the broken ripples on the surface showed jagged rocks only a few inches below. Down the middle of the channel lay our only course—and the path of the wave was narrow and the rocks harder than birch bark.

Quickly I changed places with my companion, crawling cautiously over the camping outfit stowed in the bottom, while she crept as carefully backward. In a rapids the bowsman guides the canoe, and I was the more expert. But this maneuver nearly brought disaster. A treacherous eddy just before the first pitch whirled our canoe around and we struck broadside on a boulder, where we hung, held fast by the rush of the current at the bow and stern. The edge of the canoe upstream began to settle, the water grew quickly up the side, and we avoided a spill by jumping overboard, almost up to our waists.

This, however, was only a beginning. Pulling the canoe to one side and holding it headed downstream, we stood on the rock for a breathing space while we surveyed the river, above so gentle in the sunlight, around and below so wild with the new spirit which had possessed it. Making a quick entry, with difficulty, from the rock, we again started down, steering our way where the comparatively smooth water showed the rocks well covered, working our arms till they seemed pulling from their sockets. Below us, the dashing spray, the circling eddies, the increasing clamor of the torrent, seemed to lure us as the call of a Lorelei to destruction.

The excitement of the course filled us with an ecstasy of abandon; but a sudden dash of water over the bow into our faces brought us quickly back to a sense of the danger which a moment's relaxed vigilance would bring. With every nerve alert, and guided by my previous experiences with Canadian rapids, I picked the way down the channel, my companion in the stern keeping the canoe straight with the current.

Thirty yards of fairly smooth water intervened between the upper and lower pitches, and here, somewhat awed by the spectacle of the leaping whitecaps farther down, we attempted a landing. Swinging the canoe across the current and heading for the shore which promised best, we applied our whole force to the paddles. But we had no more than half covered the distance when the futility of the effort became apparent, and we quickly turned and made in the opposite direction, where, we now discovered, the main channel lay.

Even the excitement of the adventure did not blind me to the peril which now faced us. On the lower side, as we bent our paddles to reach the channel, a row of partially submerged rocks grew ever nearer as the current drew our canoe toward them. Should we fail to reach the channel before striking, nothing human could prevent a drowning. Although a good swimmer, I could not hope to breast such waves and, escaping them, avoid the whirlpool at the foot.

With all our strength in our paddles, we lifted the light bark canoe over the water, and just as the farthest rock grated our side we swung into the channel and boiled down between the boulders, the current sweeping us on at a rate of fully fifteen miles an hour. But as we swung, my maple paddle had snapped from my hands, caught in a fissure of the rock where I had jabbed it to keep from striking.

In impotent despair I looked around at my companion. Until the present trip she never had been in a canoe, and her only knowledge in its management had been gained by my coaching and by less than two weeks of practice. But plainly the river and the forest now were in her veins, and the craft of the paddle had come by inspiration. The hesitation of the city-born was dispelled, and with skillful stroke, scarce noting my discomfiture, with eyes fixed on the winding channel ahead of us, she steered safe through the boiling waters of the second pitch. With a whirl of spray at the finish—for the rapids keeps its greatest waves for the foot, as an orator his fiercest invectives for his peroration—we brought up in the eddy below, gasping from our effort yet thrilling with the joy of it.

From

LITTLE RIVERS

Henry Van Dyke

*Henry Van Dyke (1852–1933) was an
American minister, writer, and edu-
cator.* Little Rivers, *the source of this
passage, was published in 1895.*

As we approached, the steersman in the first canoe
stood up to look over the course. The sea was
high. Was it too high? The canoes were heavily loaded.
Could they leap the waves? There was a quick talk
among the guides as we slipped along, undecided
which way to turn. Then the question seemed to settle
itself, as most of these woodland questions do, as if
some silent force of Nature had the casting-vote.
"Sautez, sautez!" cried Ferdinand, *"envoyez au large!"*
["Jump! Jump! Go forth!"] In a moment we were slid-
ing down the smooth back of the rapid, directly toward
the first big wave. The rocky shore went by us like a
dream; we could feel the motion of the earth whirling
around with us. The crest of the billow in front curled
above the bow of the canoe. *"Arrét', arrét', doucement!"*
["Take it carefully!"] A swift stroke of the paddle
checked the canoe, quivering and prancing like a horse
suddenly reined in. The wave ahead, as if surprised,
sank and flattened for a second. The canoe leaped
through the edge of it, swerved to one side, and ran
gayly down along the fringe of the line of billows, into
quieter water.

Every one feels the exhilaration of such a
descent . . . It takes a touch of danger to bring out the
joy of life.

From

"CANOEING ON THE CONNECTICUT"

John Boyle O'Reilly

John Boyle O'Reilly (1844–1890) was an athlete and writer. "Canoeing on the Connecticut" was published in Ethics of Boxing and Manly Sport.

The canoe is the American boat of the past and of the future. It suits the American mind: it is light, swift, safe, graceful, easily moved; and the occupant looks in the direction he is going, instead of behind, as in the stupid old tubs that have held the world up to this time.

Who, among the hard workers of our eastern cities, need two months' vacation, and can only get away from the desk or office for two weeks?

Who feels the confined work tell on his lungs, or his eyes, or shudders at the tremulousness of the shoulders and arms which precedes the breaking down from overwork?

All this can be cured by the sun and the wind and the delicious splash of the river on face and breast and arms. Those are they to whom a canoe is a godsend. They can get more health and strength and memorable joy out of a two-weeks' canoe trip than from a lazy, expensive and seasick voyage to Europe, or three months' dawdle at a fashionable watering place.

Boats are for work; canoes are for pleasure. Boats are artificial; canoes are natural.

From

HISTORIC WATERWAYS
SIX HUNDRED MILES OF CANOEING DOWN THE ROCK, FOX, AND WISCONSIN RIVERS

Reuben Gold Thwaites

Provided, reader, you have a goodly store of patience, stout muscles, a practiced fondness for the oars, a keen love of the picturesque and curious in nature, a capacity for remaining good-humored under the most adverse circumstances, together with a quest love for that sort of gypsy life which we call "roughing it," canoeing may be safely recommended to you as one of the most delightful and healthful of outdoor recreations, as well as one of the cheapest. . . .

The canoeist, from his lowly seat near the surface of the flood, sees the country practically as it was in pioneer days, in a state of unalloyed beauty. Each bend in the stream brings into view a new vista, and thus the bewitching scene changes as in a kaleidoscope. The people one meets, the variety of landscape one encounters, the simple adventures of the day, the sensation of being an explorer, the fresh air and simple diet, combined with that spirit of calm contentedness which overcomes the happy voyager who casts loose from care, are the never-failing attractions of such a trip. . . .

Be prepared to find canoeing a rough sport. There is plenty of hard work about it, a good deal of sunburn and blister. You will be obliged to wear your old clothes, and may not be overpleased to meet critical friends in the river towns you visit. But if you have the true spirit of the canoeist, you will win for your pains an abundance of good air, good scenery, wholesome exercise, sound sleep, and something to think about all your life.

From

"BLACK WATER AND SHALLOWS"

Frederic Remington

Frederic Remington (1861–1909) was an American artist and writer who is known for his works portraying the West. The following passage appeared in Harper's New Monthly Magazine *in 1893.*

We soon reached the head of the river, and a water-storage dam and a mile of impassable rapids made a "carry" or "portage" necessary. Slinging our packs and taking the seventy-pound canoe on our shoulders, we started down the trail. The torture of this sort of thing is as exquisitely perfect in its way as any ever devised. A trunk porter in a summer hotel simply does for a few seconds what we do by the hour, and as for reconciling this to an idea of physical enjoyment, it cannot be done. It's a subtle mental process altogether indefinable; but your enthusiast is a person who would lose all if he reasoned any, and to suffer like an anchorite is always a part of a sportsman's programme. . . . A real sportsman, of the nature-loving type, must go tramping or paddling or riding about over the waste places of the earth, with his dinner in his pocket. He is alive to the terrible strain of the "carry," and to the quiet pipe when the day is done. The campfire contemplation, the beautiful quiet of the misty morning on the still water, enrapture him, and his eye dilates, his nerves tingle, and he is a conflagration of ecstasy. When he is going—going—faster—faster into the boil of the waters, he hears the roar and boom ahead, and the black rocks crop up in thickening masses to dispute his way.

ॐॐॐ

From

"DOWN THE DELAWARE RIVER IN A CANOE"

John Boyle O'Reilly

The essay was included in Ethics of Boxing and Manly Sport.

There was no bar or ledge formation here, as in the minor rifts behind us. The rocks stood up like the broken teeth of a sperm whale, irregularly across the river, and as far ahead as we could see from the canoes. Some of the stones were twelve feet out of the water, others of lesser height, and of all shapes; some were level with the surface, and some covered with a few inches of water. These last were the dangers: to strike and get "hung up" on one of these meant certain upsetting; for no boat could stand the rush, and there was no footing for the canoeman if he tried to get out to push her over.

But more threatening than the tall rocks, that looked like a disorganized Stonehenge, was the terrible nature of the bedrock, and the broken stones on the bottom. We could steer between the teeth we saw, but we suddenly became conscious of unseen teeth that lay in wait to lacerate the boats under the waterline. . . .

From the first break of the water, the sensation was somewhat similar to that of falling through the branches of a tree. The river was twisting downhill in convulsions. We rushed through narrow slopes of ten or twenty feet as if we were falling, and then shot around a rock, flinging the whole weight of our bodies on the steering paddle. The tall stones ahead seemed to be rushing at us with the velocity of an ocean steamer.

All the time we were painfully conscious of the presence of the incisive edges underwater, as one might feel the nearness of burglars' knives in the night. If we struck one of these stones on a downward shoot, it would rip the canoe from bow to stern.

Moseley steered skillfully, and we cleared two-thirds of the tortuous descent without a shock. A quarter of a mile ahead we saw the smooth water at the foot of the rift. We had crossed the river, and were running down on the Pennsylvania shore. Suddenly, the channel we were in divided at a great white stone, the wider water going to the left, toward the center of the river, and a narrow black streak keeping straight down to the right.

A memory of the warning came to me, "Keep to the right of the big rock—if you can." But it was too late. A man could not hear his own shout in such an uproar. The white rock rushed past us. The canoes ahead had turned with the main stream, and were in the center of the river in a flash. Suddenly both canoes ahead were shot out of the channel, their bows in the air resting on a hidden rock; and the current, just then turning a sharp curve, swept by their sterns with a rush. Fortunately they were out of the stream, driven into an eddy, or that had been the end of them.

I had time to profit by their mishap. Kneeling in the canoe, using the long-handled paddle, I rounded the curve within a foot of the grounded canoes, and fairly leaped downhill on a rounded muscle of water. In the rush, a thrill swept my nerves—and another— as if twice I had touched cold steel. I found later that my canoe had twice been pierce by the knife-like edges under water.

Before I realized it, the end had come, and the canoe shot across the river in a sweeping eddy. The Great Foul Rift was behind me.

૱ૹ૱ૹ૱

From

LITTLE RIVERS

Henry Van Dyke

The real way to know a little river is not to glance at it here or there in the course of a hasty journey, nor to become acquainted with it after it has been partly civilized and spoiled by too close contact with the works of man. You must go to its native haunts; you must see it in youth and freedom; you must accommodate yourself to its pace, and give yourself to its influence, and follow its meanderings whithersoever they may lead you.

❧❧❧❧❧

From

THE MAINE WOODS

Henry David Thoreau

I will describe particularly how we got over some of these portages and rapids, in order that the reader may get an idea of the boatman's life. At Ambejijis Falls, for instance, there was the roughest path imaginable cut through the woods; at first up hill at an angle of nearly forty-five degrees, over rocks and logs without end. This was the manner of the portage:—We first carried over our baggage, and deposited it on the shore at the other end; then returning to the batteau, we dragged it up the hill by the painter, and onward, with frequent pauses, over half the portage. But this was a bungling way, and would soon have worn out the boat. Commonly, three men walk over with a batteau weighing from three to five or six hundred pounds on their heads and shoulders, the tallest standing under the middle of the boat, which is turned over, and one at each end, or else there are two at the bows. More cannot well take hold at once. But this requires some practice, as well as strength, and is in any case extremely laborious, and wearing to the constitution, to follow. We were, on the whole, rather an invalid party, and could render our boatmen but little assistance. Our two men at length took the batteau upon their shoulders and, while two of us steadied it, to prevent it from rocking and wearing into their shoulders, on which they placed their hats folded, walked bravely over the remaining distance, with two or three pauses. In the same manner they accomplished the other portages. With this crushing weight they must climb and stumble along over fallen trees and slippery rocks of all sizes, where those who walked by the sides were continually brushed off, such was the narrowness of the path. But we were fortunate not to have to cut our path in the first place. Before we launched our boat, we scraped the bottom smooth again with our knives, where it had rubbed on the rocks, to save friction.

To avoid the difficulties of the portage, our men determined to "warp up" the Passamagamet Falls: so while the rest walked over the portage with the baggage, I remained in the batteau, to assist in warping up. We were soon in the midst of the rapids, which were more swift and tumultuous than any we had poled up, and had turned to the side of the stream for the purpose of warping, when the boatmen, who felt some pride in their skill, and were ambitious to do something more than usual, for my benefit, as I surmised, took one more view of the rapids, or rather the falls; and in answer to one's question, whether we couldn't get up there, the other answered that he guessed he'd try it: so we pushed again into the midst of the stream, and began to struggle with the current. I sat in the middle of the boat, to trim it, moving slightly to the right or left as it grazed a rock. With an uncertain and wavering motion we wound and bolted our way up, until the bow was actually raised two feet above the stern at the steepest pitch; and then, when everything depended upon his exertions, the bowman's pole snapped in two; but before he had time to take the spare one, which I reached him, he had saved himself with the fragment upon a rock; and so we got up by a hair's breath; and Uncle George exclaimed, that that was never done before; and he had not tried it, if he had not known whom he had got in the bow—nor he in the bow, if he had not known him in the stern. At this place there was a regular portage cut through the woods; and our boatmen had never known a batteau to ascend the falls. As near as I can remember, there was a perpendicular fall here, at the worst place, of the whole Penobscot River, two or three feet at least. I could not sufficiently admire the skill and coolness with which they performed this feat, never speaking to each other. The bowman, not looking behind, but knowing exactly what the other is about, works as if he worked alone; now sounding in vain for a bottom in fifteen feet of water, while the boat falls back several rods, held straight only with the greatest skill and exertion; or, while the sternman obstinately holds his ground, like a turtle, the bowman springs from side to side with wonderful suppleness and dexterity, scanning the rapids and the rocks with a thousand eyes; and now, having got a bite at last, with a lusty shove which makes his pole bend and quiver, and the whole boat tremble, he gains a few feet upon the river. To add to the danger, the poles are liable at any time to be caught between the rocks, and wrenched out of their hands, leaving them at the mercy of the rapids—the rocks, as it were, lying in wait, like so many alligators, to catch them in their teeth, and jerk them from your hands, before you have stolen an effectual shove against their palates. The pole is set close to the boat,

and the prow is made to overshoot, and just turn the
corners of the rocks, in the very teeth of the rapids.
Nothing but the length and lightness, and the slight
draught of the batteau, enables them to make any
headway. The bowman must quickly choose his course;
there is no time to deliberate. Frequently the boat is
shoved between rocks where both sides touch, and the
waters on either hand are a perfect maelstrom.

Half a mile above this, two of us tried our hands at
poling up a slight rapid; and we were just surmount-
ing the last difficulty, when an unlucky rock con-
founded our calculations; and while the batteau was
sweeping round irrecoverably amid the whirlpool, we
were obliged to resign the poles to more skilful hands.

From

LIFE ON THE MISSISSIPPI

Mark Twain

Samuel Langhorne Clemens (1835–1910), an American newspaperman, humorist, travel writer, novelist, and wry political observer, took his pseudonym from his days as a steamboat pilot on the Mississippi. When the man heaving the lead in the bow called "By the mark twain," the pilot would know the water was two fathoms, or six feet, deep.

The next morning I came on with the four o'clock watch, and saw Ritchie successfully run half a dozen crossings in a fog, using for his guidance the marked chart devised and patented by Bixby himself. This sufficiently evidenced the great value of the chart.

By and by, when the fog began to clear off, I noticed that the reflection of a tree in the smooth water of an overflowed bank, six hundred yards away, was stronger and blacker than the ghostly tree itself. The faint spectral trees, dimly glimpsed through the shredding fog, were very pretty things to see.

We had a heavy thunderstorm at Natchez, another at Vicksburg, and still another about fifty miles below Memphis. They had an old-fashioned energy which had long been unfamiliar to me. This third storm was accompanied by a raging wind. We tied up to the bank when we saw the tempest coming, and everybody left the pilothouse but me. The wind bent the young trees down, exposing the pale underside of the leaves; and gust after gust followed, in quick succession, thrashing the branches violently up and down, and to this side and that, and creating swift waves of alternating green and white according to the side of the leaf that was exposed, and these waves raced after each other as do their kind over a wind-tossed field of oats. No color that was visible anywhere was quite natural—all tints were charged with a leaden tinge from the solid cloudbank overhead. The river was leaden, all distances the same; and ever the far-reaching ranks of combing whitecaps were dully shaded by the dark, rich atmosphere through which their swarming legions marched. The thunder-peals were constant and deafening; explosion followed explosion with but inconsequential intervals between, and the reports grew steadily sharper and higher-keyed, and more trying to the ear; the lightning was as diligent as the thunder, and produced effects which enchanted the eye and sent electric ecstasies of mixed delight and apprehension shivering along every nerve in the body in unintermittent procession.

The rain poured down in amazing volume; the earsplitting thunder-peals broke nearer and nearer; the wind increased in fury and began to wrench off boughs and tree-tops and send them sailing away through space; the pilothouse fell to rocking and straining and crashing and surging, and I went down in the hold to see what time it was.

People boast a good deal about Alpine thunderstorms; but the storms which I have had the luck to see in the Alps were not the equals of some which I have seen in the Mississippi Valley. I may not have seen the Alps do their best, of course, and if they can beat the Mississippi, I don't wish to.

On this up-trip I saw a little towhead (infant island) half a mile long, which had been formed during the past nineteen years. Since there was so much time to spare that nineteen years of it could be devoted to the construction of a mere towhead, where was the use, originally, in rushing this whole globe through in six days? It is likely that if more time had been taken, in the first place, the world would have been made right, and this ceaseless improving and repairing would not be necessary now. But if you hurry a world or a house, you are nearly sure to find out by and by that you have left out a towhead, or a broom-closet, or some other little convenience, here and there, which has got to be supplied, no matter how much expense or vexation it may cost.

We had a succession of black nights, going up the river, and it was observable that whenever we landed, and suddenly inundated the trees with the intense sunburst of the electric light, a certain curious effect was always produced: hundreds of birds flocked instantly out from the masses of shining green foliage, and went careering hither and thither through the white ray, and often a songbird turned up and fell to singing. We judged that they mistook this superb artificial day for the genuine article.

❧❧❧❧❧

From

ENNUI

Maria Edgeworth

Maria Edgeworth (1767–1849), a British novelist, wrote more than twenty books.

There was something in the contemplation of the sea and of the tides . . . a grand operation of nature, accompanied with a sort of vast monopoly of motion and sound which lulled me into reveries.

❧❧❧❧❧

From

MOBY DICK

Herman Melville

Moby Dick was the most memorable novel of Herman Melville (1819–1891), and has been called the greatest American novel ever written. Though it dwells on the nature of evil, it starts on a lighter note, with the narrator telling us why he goes to sea.

Call me Ishmael. Some years ago—never mind how long precisely—having little or no money in my purse, and nothing particular to interest me on the shore, I thought I would sail about a little and see the watery part of the world. It is a way I have of driving off the spleen, regulating the circulation. Whenever I find myself growing grim about the mouth; whenever it is a damp, drizzly November in my soul; whenever I find myself involuntarily pausing before coffin warehouses, and bringing up the rear of every funeral I meet; and especially whenever my hypos get such an upper hand of me, that it requires a strong moral principle to prevent me from deliberately stepping into the street, and methodically knocking people's hats off—then, I account it high time to get to sea as soon as I can. This is my substitute for pistol and ball. With a philosophical flourish Cato throws himself upon his sword; I quietly take to the ship. There is nothing surprising in this. If they but knew it, almost all men in their degree, some time or other, cherish very nearly the same feelings towards the ocean with me.

From

THE NIGGER
OF THE NARCISSUS

Joseph Conrad

*In 1897 Joseph Conrad (1857–1924)
wrote a powerful story with a title
that was, even in his less egalitarian
age, meant to catch in the throat. It
is about a person set apart from his
fellow creatures, alone with his own
despair. To isolate the character even
more, Conrad cast the whole crew
loose from the land in a smooth,
rhythmic passage of language that
has seldom been surpassed in grace.*

Next morning, at daylight, the *Narcissus* went to sea.

A slight haze blurred the horizon. Outside the harbor the measureless expanse of smooth water lay sparkling like a floor of jewels and as empty as the sky. The short black tug gave a pluck to windward, in the usual way, then let go the rope and hovered for a moment on the quarter with her engines stopped, while the slim, long hull of the ship moved ahead slowly under the lower topsails. The loose upper canvas blew out in the breeze with soft round contours, resembling small white clouds snared in the maze of ropes. Then the sheets were hauled home, the yards hoisted, and the ship became a high and lonely pyramid, gliding, all shining and white, through the sunlit mist. The tug turned short round and went away towards the land. Twenty-six pairs of eyes watched her low broad stern crawling languidly over the smooth swell between the two paddle wheels that turned fast, beating the water with fierce hurry. She resembled an enormous and aquatic black beetle, surprised by the light, overwhelmed by the sunshine, trying to escape with ineffectual effort into the distant gloom of the land. She left a lingering smudge of smoke on the sky, and two vanishing trails of foam on the water. On the place where she had stopped a round black patch of soot remained, undulating on the swell—an unclean mark of the creature's rest.

The *Narcissus,* left alone, heading south, seemed to stand resplendent and still upon the restless sea, under the moving sun. Flakes of foam swept past her sides; the water struck her with flashing blows; the land glided away slowly fading; a few birds screamed on motionless wings over the swaying mastheads. But soon the land disappeared, the birds went away; and to the west the pointed sail of an Arab dhow running for Bombay, rose triangular and upright above the sharp edge of the horizon, lingered and vanished like an illusion. Then the ship's wake, long and straight, stretched itself out through a day of immense solitude. The setting sun, burning on the level of the water, flamed crimson below the blackness of heavy rain clouds. The sunset squall, coming up from behind, dissolved itself into the short deluge of a hissing shower. It left the ship glistening from trucks to waterline, and with darkened sails. She ran easily before a fair monsoon, with her decks cleared for the night; and, moving along with her, was heard the sustained and monotonous swishing of the waves, mingled with the low whispers of men mustered aft for the setting of watches; the short plaint of some block aloft; or, now and then, a loud sigh of wind.

Mr. Baker, coming out of his cabin, called out the first name shortly before closing the door behind him. He was going to take charge on the deck. On the homeward trip, according to an old custom of the sea, the chief officer takes the first night watch—from eight till midnight. So Mr. Baker, after he had heard the last "Yes, sir!" said moodily, "Relieve the wheel and lookout"; and climbed with heavy feet the poop ladder to windward. Soon after, Mr. Creighton came down, whistling softly, and went into the cabin. On the doorstep the steward lounged, in slippers, meditative, and with his shirt sleeves rolled up to the armpits. On the main deck the cook, locking up the galley doors, had an altercation with young Charley about a pair of socks. He could be heard saying impressively, in the darkness amidships: "You don't deserve a kindness. I've been drying them for you, and now you complain about the holes—and you swear, too! Right in front of me! If I hadn't been a Christian—which you ain't, you young ruffian—I could give you a clout on the head. . . . Go away!" Men in couples or threes stood pensive or moved silently along the bulwarks in the waist. The first busy day of a homeward passage was sinking into the dull peace of resumed routine. Aft, on the high poop, Mr. Baker walked shuffling and grunted to himself in the pauses of his thoughts. Forward, the lookout man, erect between the flukes of the two anchors, hummed an endless tune, keeping his eyes fixed dutifully ahead in a vacant stare. A multitude of stars coming out into the clear night peopled the emptiness of the sky. They glittered as if alive above the sea; they surrounded the sunning ship on all sides, more intense than the eyes of a staring crowd, and as inscrutable as the souls of men.

The passage had begun and the ship, a fragment detached from the earth, went on lonely and swift like a small planet. Round her the abysses of sky and sea met in an unattainable frontier. A great circular solitude moved with her, ever changing and ever the same, always monotonous and always imposing. Now and then another wandering white speck, burdened with life, appeared far off—disappeared; intent on its own destiny. The sun looked upon her all day and every morning rose with a burning, round stare of undying curiosity. She had her own future; she was alive with the lives of those beings who trod her decks; like that earth which had given her up to the sea, she had an intolerable load of regrets and hopes. On her lived timid truth and audacious lies; and, like the earth, she was unconscious, fair to see—and condemned by men to an ignoble fate. The august loneliness of her path lent dignity to the sordid inspiration of her pilgrimage. She drove foaming to the southward, as if the sea dwarfed the extent of time. The days raced after one another, brilliant and quick like the flashes of a lighthouse, and the nights, eventful and short, resembled fleeting dreams.

The men had shaken into their places and the half-hourly voice of the bells ruled their life of unceasing care. Night and day the head and shoulders of a seaman could be seen aft by the wheel, outlined high against sunshine or starlight, very steady above the stir of revolving spokes. The faces changed, passing in rotation. Youthful faces, bearded faces, dark faces: faces serene, or faces moody, but all akin with the brotherhood of the sea; all with the same attentive expression of eyes, carefully watching the compass of the sails. Captain Allistoun, serious, and with an old red muffler round his threat, all day long pervaded the poop. At nights, many times he rose out of the darkness of the companion, such as a phantom above a grave, and stood watchful and mute under the stars, his nightshirt fluttering like a flag—then, without a sound, sank down again. He was born on the shores of the Pentland Firth. In his youth he attained the rank of harpooner in Peterhead whalers. When he spoke of that time his restless gray eyes became still and cold, like the loom of ice. Afterwards he went into the East Indian trade for the sake of change. He had commanded the *Narcissus* since she was built. He loved his ship, and drove her unmercifully; for his secret ambition was to make her accomplish some day a brilliantly quick passage which would be mentioned in nautical papers. He pronounced his owner's name with a sardonic smile, spoke but seldom to his officers, and reproved errors in a gentle voice, with words that cut to the quick. His hair was iron-gray, his face hard and the color of pump leather. He shaved every morning of his life—at six—but once (being caught in a fierce hurricane eighty miles southwest of Mauritius) he had missed three consecutive days. He feared naught but an unforgiving God, and wished to end his days in a little house, with a plot of ground attached—far in the country—out of sight of the sea.

He, the ruler of that minute world, seldom descended from the Olympian heights of his poop. Below him—at his feet, so to speak—common mortals led their busy and insignificant lives. Along the main deck, Mr. Baker grunted in a manner bloodthirsty and innocuous; and kept all our noses to the grindstone, being—as he once remarked—paid for doing that very thing. The men working about the deck were healthy and contented—as most seamen are, when once well out to sea. The true peace of God begins at any spot a thousand miles from the nearest land; and when He sends there the messengers of His might it is not in terrible wrath against crime, presumption, and folly but paternally, to chasten simple hearts—ignorant hearts that know nothing of life, and beat undisturbed by envy or greed.

᪣᪣᪣

SEASONS, DAYS, AND WEATHER

May the warp be the white light of morning,
May the weft be the red light of evening,
May the fringes be the falling rain,
May the border be the standing rainbow.
Thus weave for us a garment of brightness.

—Tewa Song of the Sky Loom

Weather does not happen. It is the visible manifestation of the Spirit moving itself in the void.

—from The Land of Little Rain
Mary Austin (1868–1934)

Screaming the night away
With his great wing feathers
Swooping the darkness up;
I hear the Eagle bird
Pulling the blanket back
Off from the eastern sky.

—Iroquois Invitation Song

The first day of spring is one thing, and the first spring day is another. The difference between them is sometimes as great as a month.

—*Henry Van Dyke*

✦✦✦

I was born with a chronic anxiety about the weather.

—*from "Is It Going to Rain?"*
John Burroughs

✦✦✦

There is a sumptuous variety about the New England weather that compels the stranger's admiration—and regret. The weather is always doing something there; always attending strictly to business; always getting up new designs and trying them on the people to see how they will go. But it gets through more business in spring than in any other season. In the spring I have counted one hundred and thirty-six different kinds of weather inside of four-and-twenty hours.

—*Speech at a dinner of the New England*
Society on December 22, 1876
Mark Twain (Samuel Langhorne Clemens)

✦✦✦

From

SIGNS AND SEASONS
John Burroughs

The critical moments of the day as regards the weather are at sunrise and sunset. A clear sunset is always a good sign; an obscured sun, just at the moment of going down after a bright day, bodes storm.

There is much truth, too, in the saying that if it rain before seven, it will clear before eleven. Nine times in ten it will turn out thus. The best time for it to begin to rain or snow, if it wants to hold out, is about mid-forenoon. The great storms usually begin at this time. On all occasions the weather is very sure to declare itself before eleven o'clock. If you are going on a picnic or are going to start on a journey, and the morning is unsettled, wait till ten and one half o'clock and you shall know what the remainder of the day will be. Midday clouds and afternoon clouds, except in the season of thunderstorms, are usually harmless idlers and vagabonds.

From

THE OREGON TRAIL

Francis Parkman

Francis Parkman (1823–1893) was a historian and horticulturalist who traveled the Oregon Trail, starting in 1846, to learn about the Indians.

But all our hopes were delusive. Scarcely had night set in, when the tumult broke forth anew. The thunder here is not like the tame thunder of the Atlantic coast. Bursting with a terrific crash directly above our heads, it roared over the boundless waste of prairie, seeming to roll around the whole circle of the firmament with a peculiar and awful reverberation. The lightning flashed all night, playing with its livid glare upon the neighboring trees, revealing the vast expanse of the plain, and then leaving us shut in as if by a palpable wall of darkness.

It did not disturb us much. Now and then a peal

awakened us, and made us conscious of the electric battle that was raging, and of the floods that dashed upon the stanch canvas over our heads. We lay upon india-rubber cloths, placed between our blankets and the soil. For a while, they excluded the water to admiration, but when at length it accumulated and began to run over the edges, they served equally well to retain it, so that toward the end of the night we were unconsciously reposing in small pools of rain.

HIGH, WIDE AND LONESOME

Hal Borland

About 1910, when Hal Borland was a boy, his parents left Nebraska to homestead on the high plains of eastern Colorado. The Wild West was a still a recent memory, and cattle ranchers, sheep herders, and homesteaders were contending for the plains. High, Wide and Lonesome *remembers those years.*

Winter ends, March drags its cold, muddy feet but finally passes, and there is Spring, a rebirth that assaults all your senses. The surge of life at the grass roots penetrates your soles, creeps up through your bones, your marrow, and right into your heart. You see it, you feel it, you smell it, you taste it in every breath you breathe. You partake of Spring. You are a part of it, even as you were a part of Winter. Spring is all around you and in you, primal, simple as the plains themselves. Spring is, and you know it.

House made of dawn,
House made of evening light,
House made of the dark cloud. . . .
Dark cloud is at the house's door,
The trail out of it is dark cloud,
The zigzag lightning stands high upon it.

—*Navaho Night Chant*
(Translated by Washington Matthews)

&

It's not raining on you—it's just raining.

— *Anonymous*

&

THE LAND

FREEWHEELIN'
A SOLO JOURNEY ACROSS AMERICA
Richard A. Lovett

*Richard Lovett left his fast-track
career in law and economics to bicycle across the country and find
another side of himself. The following passage describes the Sawtooth
Mountains in Idaho.*

Viewed from the lakeshore these mountains are the
essence of what mountains ought to be, their frac-
tured crags rising like flying buttresses on Medieval
cathedrals, culminating in spires 3,500 feet above. The
lower ridges were covered with a mantle of green, a
fuzzy shag carpet that gently blanketed their slopes
until they became too steep, and the trees gave way to
talus, granite, and remnant patches of pearly snow,
looking more pure than the puffs of clouds that deco-
rated the baby blue above the summits.

Mountains are best viewed from these lower levels, where their rocky splendor contrasts with the gentler lowlands. Mountains need room to breathe, room to survey vast regions with the remote isolation of mythical gods. For this reason I've never had the same love for the High Sierra, where jumbles of white granite are piled claustrophobically and harsh, narrow valleys hem you in until you finally scale the highest peak, with no place between the valley floor and the summit to step back and absorb the vista. In mountains like the Sawtooth I find room to appreciate the scale of the world and to wonder that the creator of all this majesty cares for me, infinitesimal speck that I am, that he is not merely like the peaks, remote in holy grandeur, but also personal and intimate like the alpine lake lapping quietly at my feet.

❧❧❧

From

THE LAND OF LITTLE RAIN

Mary Austin

Out West, the west of the mesas and the unpatented hills, there is more sky than any place in the world. It does not sit flatly on the rim of earth, but begins somewhere out in the space in which the earth is poised, hollows more, and is full of clean winey winds.

❧❧❧

To make a prairie it takes a clover and one bee,—
One clover, and a bee,
And revery.
The revery alone will do
If bees are few.

—"To Make A Prairie"
Emily Dickinson (1830–1886)

❧❧❧

From

THE EXPLORATION OF THE COLORADO RIVER AND ITS CANYONS

John Wesley Powell

John Wesley Powell and his crew knew the Grand Canyon as no one else could. Powell concluded his book, The Exploration of the Colorado River and Its Canyons, *with this passage.*

The glories and the beauties of form, color, and sound unite in the Grand Canyon—forms unrivaled even by the mountains, colors that vie with sunsets, and sounds that span the diapason from the tempest to tinkling raindrop, from cataract to bubbling fountain. But more: it is a vast district of country. Were it a valley plain it would make a state. It can be seen only in parts from hour to hour and from day to day and from week to week and from month to month. A year scarcely suffices to see it all. It has infinite variety, and no part is ever duplicated. Its colors, though many and complex at any instant, change with the ascending and declining sun; lights and shadows appear and vanish with the passing clouds, and the changing seasons mark their passage in changing colors. You cannot see the Grand Canyon in one view, as if it were a changeless spectacle from which a curtain might be lifted, but to see it you have to toil from month to month through its labyrinths. It is a region more difficult to traverse than the Alps or the Himalayas, but if strength and courage are sufficient for the task, by a year's toil a concept of sublimity can be obtained never again to be equaled on the hither side of Paradise.

From

"SPEECH AT THE GRAND CAÑON"

Theodore Roosevelt

Theodore Roosevelt (1858–1919) was the 26th president of the United States. He gave this speech in 1903.

I have come here to see the Grand Cañon of Arizona, because in that cañon Arizona has a natural wonder, which, so far as I know, is in its kind absolutely unparalleled throughout the rest of the world. I shall not attempt to describe it, because I cannot. I could not choose words that would convey or that could convey to any outsider what that canyon is. I want to ask you to do one thing in connection with it in your own interest, and in the interest of the country.

Keep this great wonder of nature as it now is.

I was delighted to learn of the wisdom of the Santa Fe Railroad in deciding not to build their hotel on the brink of the canyon. I hope you will not have a building of any kind, not a summer cottage, a hotel or anything else, to mar the wonderful grandeur, sublimity, the great loneliness and beauty of the cañon.

Leave it as it is. You cannot improve on it; not a bit. The ages have been at work on it, and man can only mar it. What you can do is to keep it for your children, your children's children and for all who come after you, as one of the great sights which every American, if he can travel at all, should see. Keep the Grand Cañon as it is.

❧❧❧

From

THE LAND OF LITTLE RAIN

Mary Austin

To underestimate one's thirst, to pass a given land-mark to the right or left, to find a dry spring where one looked for running water—there is no help for any of these things. . . .

For all the toll the desert takes of a man it gives compensations, deep breaths, deep sleep, and the communion of the stars. . . . It is hard to escape the sense of mastery as the stars move in the wide clear heavens to risings and settings unobscured. They look large and near and palpitant; as if they moved on some stately service not needful to declare. Wheeling to their stations in the sky, they make the poor world-fret of no account. Of no account you who lie out there watching, nor the lean coyote that stands off in the scrub from you and howls and howls.

❧❧❧

From

LISTENING POINT

Sigurd F. Olson

Sigurd Olson (1899–1982) was a naturalist, teacher, conservationist, and writer laureate of the North Country.

But just walking across a portage has its compensations too. In a canoe, even though you slip quietly along the shores, you still cannot achieve the feeling of intimacy that is yours on the ground. There you hear sounds that are lost on the water, see things that until then have been hidden. After hours of paddling, a

portage brings new muscles into use, and how delightful to rest with your back against the canoe, doing the
aimless things one does when there is nothing to think
about and rest is the greatest luxury on earth.

❧❧❧❧❧

From

MY NECK OF THE WOODS

Louise Dickinson Rich

*Louise Dickinson Rich and her fam-
ily left the city and moved to a rustic
cottage in western Maine. She cele-
brated country life in* We Took to the
Woods *and* My Neck of the Woods
(1950), her best-known works.

In the first place, it is very, very beautiful. It's a country of lakes and forested mountains and tumbling
rivers. It's beautiful all the time. In the spring the new
leaves of the birches and the blossoms of the maples
look like wisps of green and red smoke blowing across
the staid dark background of the fir and spruce, and
the forest floor is carpeted with flowers—huge purple
violets and tiny white ones, and the fragile wood sor-
rel, and the pink twin-sisters. The leafless rhodora
blazes in the swamps. Then the thrushes sing high on
the ridges in the arrowy light from the setting sun,
and the red deer come down the slopes, stepping dain-
tily, into the dusk of the valleys to drink. In the little
villages and cross-roads around the lofty plateau of the
lakes, the ancient lilacs break in a frenzy of bloom like
lavender surf over the low houses against which they
lean. Even when it rains—and it rains quite a lot in
Maine in the spring—it's beautiful. The curtains of the
clouds hide the mountains, and all the world is gray
and dim and full of the sound of water, and of the high,

sweet voices of the peepers in the bogs.

Summer is lovely, too, rich and full-blown. Cool, crisp nights follow blue sun-drenched days. Thunderstorms rattle around the mountains, rolling up one valley and down the next. The wild blueberries and raspberries ripen in hot clearings back in the woods, and the bear and foxes eat their fill. Everything smells wonderful—the pine, aromatic under the sun, the breeze blowing across a rock-ribbed pasture of cut hay, the very earth itself.

You have to see autumn in the North to believe it. The lakes are incredibly blue and the hillsides shout with color—orange and scarlet, yellow, and a crimson that is almost purple. In the night, the wild geese honk overhead beneath a full, burnished moon, fleeing south over the silvered ridges from the smell of winter. The Borealis crackles up from the northern horizon, sending unearthly streamers of light a thousand miles long to waver and fade at the zenith. At sunrise the ground is white with hoar-frost, against which the tracks of the rabbits and deer and bob-cats are black and precise, and the water in the ruts of the woods-road is skimmed lightly with ice. The air is like wine, thin and dry and chilled; and like wine, it exhilarates body and mind, so that the performance of great tasks and the dreaming of great dreams are as easy as turning over your hand.

And winter—what can I say about winter, when the wind, clean and knife-edged, pours down from the northwest, and the country is held in the grip of an iron cold? The snow falls and falls, steadily and soundlessly; or it drives down the bitter wind, scourging the land. The houses in the villages huddle together like sheep under its lash. The ice on the lakes silently thickens—one foot, eighteen inches, three feet—until it is as solid as living ledge under the heaviest load. In the dead silence of a windless night, it surrenders to the strain of its own increasing pressure, and as the rift runs across a lake—two, four, ten miles—a great half-human howl echoes through the mountains and up to the stars. It's a blood-chilling sound to hear, wild and lost and despairing.

From

A LADY'S LIFE IN THE ROCKY MOUNTAINS

Isabella L. Bird

Isabella Bird was an Englishwoman who ignored Victorian mores. She traveled throughout Canada and the United States and explored the Rockies on horseback.

There no lumberer's axe has ever rung. The trees die when they have attained their prime, and stand there, dead and bare, till the fierce mountain winds lay them prostrate. The pines grew smaller and more sparse as we ascended, and the last stragglers wore a tortured, warring look. The timber line was passed, but yet a little higher a slope of mountain meadow dipped to the south-west towards a bright stream trickling under ice and icicles, and there a grove of the beautiful silver spruce marked our camping ground. The trees were in miniature, but so exquisitely arranged that one might well ask what artist's hand had planted them, scattering them here, clumping them there, and training their slim spires towards heaven.

❧❧❧❧❧

From

"THE LEGEND OF SLEEPY HOLLOW"

Washington Irving

Washington Irving (1783–1859), an American writer, created the character Ichabod Crane in "The Legend of Sleepy Hollow."

It was, as I have said, a fine autumnal day, the sky was clear and nature wore that rich and golden livery which we always associate with the idea of abundance. The forests had put on their sober brown and yellow, while some trees of the tenderer kind had been nipped by the frosts into brilliant dyes of orange, purple, and scarlet. Streaming files of wild ducks began to make their appearance high in the air; the bark of the squirrel might be heard from the groves of beech and hickory nuts, and the pensive whistle of the quail at intervals from the neighboring stubble-field.

The small birds were taking their farewell banquets. In the fulness of their revelry, they fluttered, chirping and frolicking, from bush to bush, and tree to tree, capricious from the very profusion and variety around them. There was the honest cockrobin, the favorite game of stripling sportsmen, with its loud querulous notes; and the twittering blackbirds flying in sable clouds; and the golden-winged woodpecker, with his crimson crest, his broad black gorget, and splendid plumage; and the cedar-bird, with its red-tipt wings and yellow-tipt tail, and its little montiero cap of feathers; and the blue jay, that noisy coxcomb, in his gray light-blue coat and white under-clothes, screaming and chattering, nodding and bobbing and bowing, and pretending to be on good terms with every songster of the grove.

As Ichabod jogged slowly on his way, his eye, ever open to every symptom of culinary abundance, ranged with delight over the treasures of jolly autumn. On all sides he beheld vast stores of apples; some hanging in oppressive opulence on the trees; some gathered into baskets and barrels for the market; others heaped up in rich piles for the cider-press. Farther on he beheld great fields of Indian corn, with its golden ears peeping from their leafy coverts, and holding out the promise of cakes and hasty-pudding; and the yellow pumpkins lying beneath them, turning up their fair round bellies to the sun, and giving ample prospects of the most luxurious of pies; and anon he passed the fragrant buckwheat fields, breathing the odor of the bee-hive, and as he beheld them, soft anticipations stole over his mind of dainty slapjacks, well buttered, and garnished with honey or treacle, by the delicate little dimpled hand of Katrina Van Tassel.

Thus feeding his mind with many sweet thoughts and "sugared suppositions," he journeyed along the sides of a range of hills which look out upon some of the goodliest scenes of the mighty Hudson. The sun gradually wheeled his broad disk down into the west. The wide bosom of the Tappan Zee lay motionless and

glossy, excepting that here and there a gentle undula-
tion waved and prolonged the blue shadow of the distant mountain. A few amber clouds floated in the sky,
without a breath of air to move them. The horizon was
of a fine golden tint, changing gradually into a pure
apple-green, and from that into the deep blue of the
mid-heaven. A slanting ray lingered on the woody
crests of the precipices that overhung some parts of
the river, giving greater depth to the dark-gray and
purple of their rocky sides. A sloop was loitering in the
distance, dropping slowly down with the tide, her sail
hanging uselessly against the mast; and as the reflection of the sky gleamed along the still water, it seemed
as if the vessel was suspended in the air.

FELLOW CREATURES

DESERT SOLITAIRE
A SEASON IN THE WILDERNESS

Edward Abbey

Edward Abbey wrote Desert Solitaire *after working as a seasonal ranger in Arches National Monument (now a national park) in southeast Utah.*

Why do they sing? What do they have to sing about? Somewhat apart from one another, separated by roughly equal distances, facing outward from the water, they clank and croak all through the night with a tireless perseverance. To human ears their music has a bleak, dismal, tragic quality, dirgelike rather than jubilant. It may nevertheless be the case that these small beings are singing not only to claim their stake in the pond, not only to attract a mate, but also out of spontaneous love and joy, a contrapuntal choral celebration of the coolness and wetness after weeks of desert fire, for love of their own existence, however brief it may be, and for joy in the common life.

Has joy any survival value in the operations of evolution? I suspect that it does; I suspect that the morose and fearful are doomed to quick extinction. Where there is no joy there can be no courage; and without courage all other virtues are useless. Therefore the frogs, the toads, keep on singing even though we know, if they don't, that the sound of their uproar must surely be luring all the snakes and ring-tail cats and kit foxes and coyotes and great horned owls toward the scene of their happiness.

❧❧❧

Out of the earth
I sing for them
a Horse nation . . .
I sing for them
the animals.

—"I Sing for the Animals"
Teton Sioux song

❧❧❧

What is man without the beasts? If all the beasts were gone, men would die from great loneliness of spirit, for whatever happens to the beasts also happens to the man.

—Seattle (1786?–1866), Chief of the Dwamish
and allied tribes of Puget Sound

❧❧❧

Two may talk together under the same roof for many years, yet never really meet; and two others at first speech are old friends.

—"Marianson" in Mackinac and Lake Stories
Mary Catherwood (1847–1902)

❧❧❧

From

DANGEROUS RIVER

R. M. Patterson

The next day was one of blazing sunshine and joyous venture on the river, winding up with an unseemly fracas in camp at suppertime. Camp, that evening, was under the cottonwoods on a sandy beach in an eddy at the foot of some fairly strong water. Immediately behind was a low cliff, the continuation of a canyon wall, and the beach came to an end a few yards below camp, against the cliff and at the head of a riffle. I made a long, double-log fire halfway between the water and the cliff, and on it I sat several pots— tea water, washing water, prunes and rice, and the mulligan pot with the last of the moose soup in it and a couple of partridges in the soup. Then I threw my bedroll down by a big spruce at the foot of the cliff, took off a soaking wet shirt and hung it on a tree to dry and went to bail the canoe which had shipped water on the last crossing of the river.

As I bailed I heard a grunting noise from upstream: a cow moose and her calf were swimming the river; the calf was having a tough time of it in the fast water, and the cow was talking to it and encouraging it. She probably intended to land where I had beached the canoe, but she saw me and headed straight for the bank, landing about a hundred yards upstream. The calf, however, had been doing its utmost and had nothing in reserve: it was swept downriver and into the eddy, from which it splashed ashore about fifteen yards below camp.

I was in the classic situation—in between mother and child; and mother weighed about eight hundred pounds, and a decidedly querulous note was creeping into her grunts. The calf let out a feeble bleat, and the cow came a little closer, grunting angrily: I waded ashore and gently took down the rifle from a tree close to the canoe where it was hanging. Then I waded into the river to see if I could get around the calf and chase it back upstream to its mother: out of the corner of my eye I could see that the soup was boiling over; the tea pail also had a fine head of steam up, and no doubt the rice was burning—and I silently cursed the whole tribe of moose right back to its remote beginnings. Anything but a prehistoric-looking beast like that would have had sense enough to stay out of camp!

I was in the water now, as deep as I could get, the rifle held high in one hand and the other busily engaged in unknotting the red silk scarf that was around my neck. The calf was watching me: heaven send the little fool wouldn't lose his head and take off down the canyon and get himself drowned; if he did the cow would blame it all on me and come charging through camp and wreck everything—and stop a bullet, when all I wanted was peace. But the calf never moved, and I came dripping out of the river below him and walked up the bank. He seemed to be petrified: not so the cow, however. She was working herself into a fine frenzy and pawing at the sand—a bad sign, that. It was high time to get that calf on the move.

I came right up behind him, flapped the red scarf suddenly and let out one devil of a yell. I had intended to fire a shot over him as well, just to speed him on his way but there was no need for that—he was already going faster than mortal moose calf had ever gone before. And how perfectly it was all working out! He would pass between my bedroll and the fire; no damage would be done, and there would still be time for me to salvage something of my supper from the ruins of what might have been. . . .

But how completely the picture changed, all in a fraction of a second! Just as the calf drew level with it a little breeze from the west flapped the shirt that was drying on the tree: he gave a blat of terror and shied sideways, stumbling over the long logs of the fire. Over went everything, but particularly the mulligan pot which he sent flying ahead with his front feet. He then bucked over the fire and landed with one hind foot through the stout bail handle of the mulligan pot, which somehow stayed with him for about three jumps and then, as he freed himself from it with a vicious kick, sailed into the river, from which I rescued it. That was the end of the party, and judging by the row that came from up the beach, the guests were leaving in a hurry. Supper was a wreck, the partridge mulligan had gone down the river, and the calf had pretty nearly squared the pot for me; I spent half the night hammering it round again with the back of an axe.

⟡⟡⟡

The buffaloes are gone.
And those who saw the buffaloes are gone.
Those who saw the buffaloes by thousands and how they pawed the prairie sod into dust with their hoofs, their great heads down pawing on in a great pageant of dusk.
Those who saw the buffaloes are gone.
And the buffaloes are gone.

—"Buffalo Dusk"
Carl Sandburg (1878–1967)

⟡⟡⟡

From

A SAND COUNTY ALMANAC AND SKETCHES HERE AND THERE

Aldo Leopold

In 1909, Aldo Leopold joined the U.S. Forest Service as a ranger in Arizona and New Mexico. The killing of the wolf reflects his training and the prevailing attitude at that time. Over the years, his work shifted from game management to an appreciation of the complexity of ecology and he became an influential nature essayist.

In those days we had never heard of passing up a chance to kill a wolf. In a second we were pumping lead into the pack, but with more excitement than accuracy: how to aim a steep downhill shot is always confusing. When our rifles were empty, the old wolf was down, and a pup was dragging a leg into impassable slide-rocks.

We reached the old wolf in time to watch a fierce green fire dying in her eyes. I realized then, and have known ever since, that there was something new to me in those eyes—something known only to her and to the mountain. I was young then, and full of trigger-itch; I thought that because fewer wolves meant more deer, that no wolves would mean hunters' paradise. But after seeing the green fire die, I sensed that neither the wolf nor the mountain agreed with such a view.

ADVERSITY

NORTHERN NURSE

Elliott Merrick

For a few miles the snow bore up our runners, and at sunrise, a beauty with oceans of colored cloud fields, we were a long way out on the bay. A blue haze crept over all the shores. The dogs began to sink, the runners stuck and great clogging lumps formed on the front of the sledge. It crunched slowly from length to length like an inch-worm measuring itself. We had to walk to lighten the load, and the walking was terrific with snowshoes on, and impossible without. When we left our first boil-up place, we each took with us a stick for knocking our overshoes, but even so, they were heavy. Lifting that extra weight stretches a muscle in the thigh and gives one what the voyageurs used to call *mal de raquette*. Nobody knows how small a person seems and how big the bay, when the team crawls and the walking is heavy. You might as well set out walking to the moon as toward the next point. It was slow and we were sweating. We wished it were twenty below again so we could travel fast and be dry and comfortable. Three times we stopped for bread and tea, and each time the breeze seemed cold, our backs shivery, our feet clammy, our mittens soggy.

From

LIBBY
THE ALASKAN DIARIES AND LETTERS OF LIBBY BEAMAN, 1879–1880, AS PRESENTED BY HER GRANDDAUGHTER, BETTY JOHN

Libby Beaman

Libby Beaman accompanied her husband to the Alaskan Pribilof Islands, just outside the Arctic Circle, in 1879.

March 26, St. Paul, Pribilof Group
Dearest Ones,
The deep black night of winter has been with us a long time. Unless one lives in it, one cannot imagine the few hours of half-light we now begin to see. Of course, there is no sun yet. The rest of the time it is very dark, indeed, except for an occasional fearful display of the northern lights, so overwhelmingly beautiful that one is afraid to look at them. Never in the recorded history of the island has there been such a severe winter. Following last winter's mild weather, this comes as something of a shock. Last year the natives suffered from the mild weather. This year we all suffer from the extreme cold. We suffer many hardships because all our meat is in the cold shed, under tons of ice which we cannot budge.

Fortunately, early in the fall before the snows

came, we laid in ample supplies of everything we might need in case we could not get down to the Lodge. The bad weather set in early. But it abated at Christmastime and continued fairly mild into January. My idea of mild and yours are far different. Our idea of mild means bearable. After the holidays, about which I've written you, I resumed teaching school and thought the worst of the winter was over. But Mr. Redpath insisted that we lay in more supplies against another storm. Thank goodness we did, although there was not much to choose from. Our diet now has been reduced to tea and starchy foods.

This week has been the worst of all weeks, more than six weeks of being housebound! We have rationed ourselves to our few remaining stocks of food. I think when one is denied something, that is what one wants most. Right now I crave dried prunes! Can you imagine it? As I write this, they seem the ultimate of the unobtainable. In fact, we'll not see a dried prune until May, when the *St. Paul* gets here. I am glad that by the time you read this our ordeal will be past. A ship will have brought us the supplies we need. They will seem like the greatest luxuries.

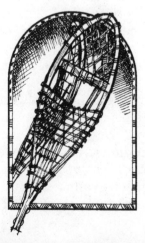

Adversity is the first path to Truth.

—*from* Don Juan
George Gordon Byron (1788–1824)

ଵ❦ଵ❦ଵ❦

By trying we can easily learn to endure adversity. Another man's, I mean.

—*from* "Pudd'nhead Wilson's New Calendar,"
in Following the Equator
Mark Twain

Courage is resistance to fear, mastery of fear—not absence of fear.

—*from* Pudd'nhead Wilson
Mark Twain

ଵ❦ଵ❦ଵ❦

From

THE EXPLORATION OF THE COLORADO RIVER AND ITS CANYONS

John Wesley Powell

These two passages describe the challenges that John Wesley Powell and his men faced while navigating whitewater in the Grand Canyon just above and below the confluence of the Little Colorado and Colorado rivers.

August 5—With some feeling of anxiety we enter a new canyon this morning. We have learned to observe closely the texture of the rock. In softer strata we have a quiet river, in harder we find rapids and falls. Below us are the limestones and hard sandstones which we found in Cataract Canyon. This bodes toil and danger. Besides the texture of the rocks, there is another condition which affects the character of the channel, as we have found by experience. Where the strata are horizontal the river is often quiet, and, even though it may be very swift in places, no great obstacles are found. Where the rocks incline in the direction traveled, the river usually sweeps with great velocity, but still has few rapids and falls. But where the rocks dip up stream and the river cuts obliquely across the upturned formations, harder strata above and softer below, we have rapids and falls. Into hard rocks and into rocks dipping up stream we pass this morning and start on a long, rocky, mad rapid. On the left there is a vertical rock, and down by this cliff and around to the left we glide, tossed just enough by the waves to appreciate the rate at which we are traveling. . . .

August 15—It is not easy to describe the labor of such navigation. We must prevent the waves from dashing the boats against the cliffs. Sometimes, where the river is swift, we must put a bight of rope about a rock, to prevent the boat from being snatched from us by a wave; but where the plunge is too great or the chute too swift, we must let her leap and catch her below or the undertow will drag her under the falling water and sink her. Where we wish to run her out a little way from shore through a channel between rocks, we first throw in little sticks of driftwood and watch their course, to see where we must steer so that she will pass the channel in safety. And so we hold, and let go, and pull, and lift, and ward—among rocks, around rocks, and over rocks.

From

DESERT SOLITAIRE
A SEASON IN THE WILDERNESS

Edward Abbey

Long before I reached the place where I could descend safely to the main canyon and my camp, however, darkness set in, the clouds opened their bays and the rain poured down. I took shelter under a ledge in a shallow cave about three feet high—hardly room to sit up in. Others had been there before: the dusty floor of the little hole was littered with the droppings of birds, rats, jackrabbits and coyotes. There were also a few long gray pieces of scat with a curious twist at one tip—cougar? I didn't care. I had some matches with me, sealed in paraffin (the prudent explorer); I scraped together the handiest twigs and animal droppings and built a little fire and waited for the rain to stop.

It didn't stop. The rain came down for hours in alternate waves of storm and drizzle and I very soon had burnt up all the fuel within reach. No matter. I stretched out in the coyote den, pillowed my head on my arm and suffered through the long long night, wet, cold, aching, hungry, wretched, dreaming claustrophobic nightmares. It was one of the happiest nights of my life.

❧❧❧

People don't ever seem to realize that doing what's right's no guarantee against misfortune.

—*from* Casuals of the Sea
William McFee (1881–1966)

❧❧❧

From

A WOMAN'S JOURNEY ON THE APPALACHIAN TRAIL

Cindy Ross

Soon the rain creeps into every corner of my body. It runs in streams down my poncho, onto my legs, saturates my socks and collects in my boots. And collects. And collects, until I'm walking on sponges and water squirts out of the pores of the leather, and I must stop every 15 minutes to wring my socks out, getting nearly a half-cup of water every time.

My nose runs constantly. My hair is plastered to my face. There is dirt everywhere on me. Little pieces of leaves and bark stick to my wet skin like magnets.

I'm cold. I'm wet. I'm numb and hungry because I can't stop to eat or rest or I'll freeze and all I can think of is *home!*

But something must be said for the joys of rain. On those unearthly mornings when I awake and the land is swimming in a warm, misty, opaque fog. Moisture hangs onto everything; every leaf, every branch, every dust particle in the atmosphere. It holds it there until it can't hold anymore and lets go drop by drop, clinging to my eyelashes, thickening my hair, moistening my skin and I'm glad I'm alive and moving through it.

From

THE LURE OF
THE LABRADOR WILD

Dillon Wallace

After Leonidas Hubbard, Dillon Wallace, and George Elson abandoned their goal of Lake Michikamau in Labrador, they found themselves in a desperate race for survival.

We pitched the tent facing a big rock so that the heat from the fire, blazing between, might be reflected into the tent, the front of which was thrown wide open. Of course George and I did all the camp work. Fortunately there was not much to do; our camps being pitched on the sites of previous ones, we had stakes ready to hand for the tent, and in this part of the country we were able to find branches and logs that we could burn without cutting. We still had one axe with us, but neither George nor I had the strength to swing it.

The night was cold and damp. For supper we had another piece of the caribou hide, and water from the much-boiled bones with what I believed was the last of the pea meal—about two spoonfuls that Hubbard shook into the pot from the package, which he then threw away. As we reclined in the open front of the tent before the fire, I again read from the Bible, and again a feeling of religious exaltation came to Hubbard. "I'm so happy, and oh! so sleepy," he murmured, and was quiet. He did not make his usual entry in his diary. In my own diary for this date I find:

"Hubbard's condition is pitiable, but he bears himself like the hero that he is—trying always to cheer and encourage us. He is visibly failing. His voice is very weak and low. I fear he will break down at every step. O God, what can we do! How can we save him!"

On Saturday (October 17) threatening clouds overcast the sky, and a raw wind was blowing. It penetrated our rags and set us a-shiver. At dawn we had more water from the bones and more of the hide. Cold and utterly miserable, we forced our way along. Our progress was becoming slower and slower. But every step was taking us nearer home, we said, and with that thought we encouraged ourselves. At noon we came upon our first camp above the Susan River. There George picked up one of our old flour bags. A few lumps of moldy flour were clinging to it, and he scraped them carefully into the pot to give a little substance to the bone water. We also found a box with a bit of baking powder still in it. The powder was streaked with rust from the tin, but we ate it all.

Then Hubbard made a find—a box nearly half full of pasty mustard. After we had each eaten a mouthful, George put the remainder in the pot. He was about to throw the box away when Hubbard asked that it be returned to him. Hubbard took the box and sat holding it in his hand.

"That box came from Congers," he said, as if in a reverie. "It came from my home in Congers. Mina has had this very box in her hands. It came from the little grocery store where I've been so often. Mina handed it to me before I left home. She said the mustard might be useful for plasters. We've eaten it instead. I wonder where my girl is now. I wonder when I'll see her again. Yes, she had that very box in her hands—in *her* hands! She's been such a good wife to me."

Slowly he bent his head, and the tears trickled down his cheeks.

George and I turned away.

It is the first shower that wets.

—*Italian proverb*

Prosperity is not without many fears and dis-
tastes;
and adversity is not without comforts and hopes.

—*from "Of Adversity," in* Essays
Francis Bacon (1561–1626)

A great wind is blowing, and that gives you either
imagination or a headache.

—*from a letter to Baron F. M. Grimm, April 29, 1775*
Catherine II, also known as Catherine the Great

THE NATURE OF THINGS

What is life? It is the flash of a firefly in the night. It is the breath of a buffalo in the wintertime. It is the little shadow which runs across the grass and loses itself in the sunset.

—Last words
Crowfoot (1821–1890)

PRAIRIE WATERS BY NIGHT

Carl Sandburg

Chatter of birds two by two raises a night song joining
   a litany of running water—sheer waters showing
   the russet of old stones remembering many rains.

And the long willows drowse on the shoulders of the
   running water, and sleep from much music joined
   songs of day-end, feathery throats and stony
   waters, in a choir chanting new psalms.

It is too much for the long willows when low laughter

of a red moon comes down; and the willows drowse and sleep on the shoulder of the running water.

❧❧❧

From

LETTERS ON AN ELK HUNT

Elinore Pruitt Stewart

This work was published in 1915, two years after Letters of a Woman Homesteader.

Dawn in the mountains—how I wish I could describe it to you! If I could only make you feel the keen, bracing air, the exhilarating climb; if I could only paint its beauties, what a picture you should have! Here the colors are very different from those of the desert. I suppose the forest makes it so. The shadows are mellow, like the colors in an old picture—greenish amber light and a blue-gray sky. Far ahead of us we could see the red rim rock of a mountain above timber line. The first rays of the sun turned the jagged peaks into golden points of a crown. In Oklahoma, at that hour of the day, the woods would be alive with song-birds, even at this season; but here there are no song-birds, and only the snapping of twigs, as our horses climbed the frosty trail, broke the silence.

❧❧❧

From

REFLECTIONS FROM THE NORTH COUNTRY

Sigurd F. Olson

I have traveled [alone] as my friend did many times, and while I love to have companions with me, I discovered long ago what psychologists call "creative silence": the impact of solitude on the mind, the awakening of ideas and thoughts normally hidden when one is with others, the emergence of concepts often lost owing to interruptions and responsibilities. During such times, one drinks from the deep wells of the past.

Something I have often done is to take a bit of poetry or philosophy out of my medicine bag, as I call it, fragments gathered over the years, lay it on a pack before me anchored firmly with a stone, and read it line by line, with time enough to savor every word. This is the way reading should be done, but there is seldom unbroken time or lack of interference that shatters one's absorption. . . . Paddling along watching the skies, clouds, and horizons, there is time to mull such thoughts deeply and translate them not in one's own mind, but in the timeless background of hills and distance, the eternal and the immutable.

Everyone needs such quiet times, some solitude to recoup his sense of perspective. One does not have to be in a canoe or in some remote wilderness. I find such times at night when I do much of my reading, but to me when solitude is part of wilderness it comes more surely and with greater meaning. Since the time when man often traveled alone, hunting and foraging, all this became part of him. It is easy to slip back into the ancient grooves of experience.

❧❧❧❧

Nature teaches more than she preaches. There are no sermons in stones. It is easier to get a spark out of a stone than a moral.

—*from* Time and Change
John Burroughs

❧❧❧❧

From

THE HILLS OF HINGHAM

Dallas Lore Sharp

*Dallas Lore Sharp (1870–1929) was
an American professor of English
who wrote essays about nature.*

But how sweet is the silence! To be so far removed from sounds that one can hear a single cricket and the creeping of a beetle in the leaves! Life allows so little margin of silence nowadays. One cannot sit down in quiet and listen to the small voices; one is obliged to stand up—in a telephone booth, a pitiful, two-by-two oasis of silence in life's desert of confusion and din. If October brought one nothing else but this sweet refuge from noises it would be enough. For the silence of October, with its peculiar qualities, is pure balm. There is none of the oppressive stillness that precedes a severe storm, none of the ominous hush that falls before the first frost, none of the death-like lack of sound in a bleak snow-buried swamp or pasture, none of the awesome majesty of quiet in the movement of the midnight stars, none of the fearful dumbness of the desert, that muteness without bound or break, eternal—none of these qualities in the sweet silence of October. I have listened to all of these, and found them answering to mute tongues within my own soul, deep unto deep; but such moods are rare—moods that can meet death, that can sweep through the heavens with the constellations, and that can hold converse with the dumb, stirless desert; whereas the need for the healing and restoration found in the serene silence of October is frequent.

From

THE WINTER BEACH

Charlton Ogburn, Jr.

No sensible person would, either, have us "return to nature," to be as the American Indian was, much as one may esteem him. If there were no towns, my hand, surely, would be among the first raised in favor of having them. Again I think it is a matter of balance. And the balance would seem now to be tipped very far to the side of the machinery of civilization. The give-and-take relationship between men and their natural setting, by which each is shaped by the other and acquires something of the other's character, is for the West clearly a thing of the past. The equilibrium has been upset. Increasingly man imposes his ways on nature and is less and less affected by nature or—to put it another way—receives less and less from nature.

❧❧❧

From

LIBBY

THE ALASKAN DIARIES AND LETTERS OF LIBBY BEAMAN, 1879–1880, AS PRESENTED BY HER GRANDDAUGHTER, BETTY JOHN

Libby Beaman

Last night before going to bed, we stood thus at the window when suddenly the aurora borealis sprang up from the far waters of the Bering like a rainbow of promise. According to everyone who has seen the northern lights from Alaska or Canada, our northern lights are not very spectacular. We don't often have them. But they have always been beautiful to me. This time, the aurora was a tremendous display, fascinating, awe inspiring, and a little frightening. Great diaphanous curtains of colored light opened and closed the proscenium arch of the heavens. Whole ballets of darting, leaping, flying light fairies danced across the stage, back and forth, changing colors, changing shape, merging with the vast curtains, then scurrying away like quicksilver, an endless variation of themes and rhythms. We could not leave the window, though we grew numb with cold. It was as though the hand of God were improvising on an organ of light and giving us a sign of His presence. Or was He trying to show us how beautiful heaven is?

ตตตต

Simple and fresh and fair from winter's close emerging,
As if no artifice of fashion, business, politics, had ever been,
Forth from its sunny nook of shelter'd grass—innocent, golden, calm as the dawn,
The spring's first dandelion shows its trustful face.

—"The First Dandelion"
Walt Whitman

ตตตต

The West of which I speak is but another name for
the Wild; and what I have been preparing to say is,
that in Wildness is the preservation of the World.

—from "Walking"
Henry David Thoreau

From

HIGH, WIDE AND LONESOME

Hal Borland

I lay there thinking about the beetles and the ants
and the prairie dogs and the badgers and the owls
and the meadow larks. They had been here a long
time, all of them. They were here when the buffalo
first came, and that was so long ago that the Indians
couldn't remember that far back. Time was a strange
thing. It was days and nights and months and years,
and then it stretched out into something else. Into
grass, maybe, or into clouds. Or into the earth itself.
You lay watching a cloud overhead, and you closed
your eyes and pretty soon the cloud moved over the
sun. You felt the coolness and the darkness of the
shadow. You lay and waited for the brightness and the
sun's warmth again. You could count, slowly, and that
was time. You counted slowly, and the cloud passed the
sun. The shadow was gone.

Time was strange. A prairie dog pup was born in
May, and by Fall it was practically grown up. A
meadow lark laid an egg in a nest in May and before
frost in the Fall the baby bird hatched from that egg
was as big as its mother and it flew south with the
other birds. But it took years for a boy to grow up.

We had been out there two years. When we first
came I was so short I had to stand on a manger or a
cut-bank to get on a horse. Now I could mount Mack

from the ground, just put my hands on his withers and jump and throw my leg over his back.

I wondered how many ants had grown old and died while I was growing up enough to get on a horse from the ground. A year must be a long time to an ant. Or a beetle. Or a prairie dog. Even a day must be a long time. Maybe time was like distance. If an ant got twenty feet away from the ant hill he was a long way from home, much farther than I was right now from the house. And it probably would take a tumblebug all day to roll that ball of dung fifty feet, especially with all the obstacles it had to get over or around.

❦❦❦

From

A SAND COUNTY ALMANAC AND SKETCHES HERE AND THERE

Aldo Leopold

The song of a river ordinarily means the tune that waters play on rock, root, and rapid. . . . This song of the waters is audible to every ear, but there is other music in these hills, by no means audible to all. To hear even a few notes of it you must first live here for a long time, and you must know the speech of hills and rivers. Then on a still night, when the campfire is low and the Pleiades have climbed over rimrocks, sit quietly and listen for a wolf to howl, and think hard of everything you have seen and tried to understand. Then you may hear it—a vast pulsing harmony—its score inscribed on a thousand hills, its notes the lives and deaths of plants and animals, its rhythms spanning the seconds and the centuries.

❦❦❦

Lovely! See the cloud, the cloud appear!
Lovely! See the rain, the rain draw near!
Who spoke?
It was the little corn ear
High on the tip of the stalk.

—*Zuni corn-grinding song*

❧❧❧❧

The eye of the trilobite tells us that the sun shone
on the old beach where he lived; for there is nothing in
nature without a purpose, and when so complicated an
organ was made to receive the light, there must have
been light to enter it.

—*from* Geological Sketches
Jean Louis Rodolphe Agassiz (1807–1873)

❧❧❧❧

From

LAND OF THE SPOTTED EAGLE

Luther Standing Bear of the Sioux

Only to the white man was nature a "wilderness"
and only to him was the land "invested" with
"wild" animals and "savage" people. To us it was tame.
Earth was bountiful and we were surrounded by the
blessings of the Great Mystery. Not until the hairy
man from the east came and with brutal frenzy
heaped injustices upon us and the families that we
loved was it "wild" for us. When the very animals of
the forest began fleeing from his approach, then it was
that for us the "Wild West" began.

❧❧❧❧

From

IN DEFENSE OF NATURE

John Hay

Conservation, along with world poverty, ought to get all the support that is reserved for war and supersonic jets; but there are times when I wonder what the term means, or if its meaning has not been so dimmed by public usage that it has lost some of its efficacy in the process. Because conservation is in the public domain, it runs the political risk of having too many faces and facing in too many different directions. The basic question is what we think it important to conserve, and if we can only answer that in terms of our own economic and technological demands we may find that we have left out most of earth and our own sustenance. How can we put our overwhelming utilitarian world, with all its automatic functions, in the right relation with an earth whose provenance and integrity it disregards? If it is our intention to save open space, will it be saved for its own sake or for "public use," and how do you define what the public needs in any other terms than those of public pressure?

It is very difficult, and often justifiably so, to make people believe in a balanced alliance between them and the natural world when they feel that their own wants and livelihood might be impaired by it. We have not been effectively persuaded that our livelihood, even our sanity, depends on a natural environment which is allowed its own proper growth and functions. We have not been taught that our replacements of ecological systems have on the whole left the world much poorer than it used to be. We have not been educated in the fact that our livelihood depends not only on the conservation of open areas but on recognition of the diverse standards of natural existence everywhere, without exception.

LITTLE RIVERS

Henry Van Dyke

A river is the most human and companionable of all inanimate things. It has a life, a character, a voice of its own, and is as full of good fellowship as a sugar-maple is of sap. It can talk in various tones, loud or low, and of many subjects, grave and gay. Under favourable circumstances it will even make a shift to sing, not in a fashion that can be reduced to notes and set down in black and white on a sheet of paper, but in a vague, refreshing manner, and to a wandering air that goes

"Over the hills and far away."

For real company and friendship, there is nothing outside of the animal kingdom that is comparable to a river.

I will admit that a very good case can be made out in favour of some other objects of natural affection. For example, a fair apology has been offered by those ambitious persons who have fallen in love with the sea. But, after all, that is a formless and disquieting passion. It lacks solid comfort and mutual confidence. The sea is too big for loving, and too uncertain. It will not fit into our thoughts. It has no personality because it has so many. It is a salt abstraction. You might as well think of loving a glittering generality like "the American woman." One would be more to the purpose.

Mountains are more satisfying because they are more individual. It is possible to feel a very strong attachment for a certain range whose outline has grown familiar to our eyes, or a clear peak that has looked down, day after day, upon our joys and sorrows, moderating our passions with its calm aspect. We

come back from our travels, and the sight of such a
well-known mountain is like meeting an old friend
unchanged. But it is a one-sided affection. The mountain is voiceless and imperturbable; and its very lofti-
ness and serenity sometimes make us the more lonely.

❧❧❧

Now I see the secret of making the
best persons,
It is to grow in the open air and to
eat and sleep with the earth.

—from "Song of the Open Road"
Walt Whitman

❧❧❧

The toe of the star-gazer is often stubbed.

—Russian proverb

❧❧❧

From

THE JOURNALS OF
LEWIS AND CLARK

Meriwether Lewis

August 18, 1805: This day I completed my thirty
first year, and conceived that I had in all human
probability now existed about half the period which I
am to remain in this Sublunary world. I reflected that
I had as yet done but little, very little, indeed, to fur-
ther the happiness of the human race or to advance
the information of the succeeding generation. I viewed
with regret the many hours I have spent in indolence,
and now soarly feel the want of that information which
those hours would have given me had they been judi-

ciously expended. But since they are past and cannot be recalled, I dash from me the gloomy thought, and resolved in future, to redouble my exertions and at least indeavour to promote those two primary objects of human existence, by giving them the aid of that portion of talents which nature and fortune have bestoed on me; or in future, to live for *mankind*, as I have heretofore lived *for myself*.

From

THE HILLS OF HINGHAM

Dallas Lore Sharp

Perhaps I have never seen life whole; I may need a throne and not a hill and a stump for that; but here in the wideness of the open skies, in the sweet quiet, in the hush that often fills these deep woods, I sometimes see life free, not free from men and things, but unencumbered, coming to meet me out of the morning and passing on with me toward the sunset until, at times, the stepping westward, the uneventful onwardness of life has

". . . seemed to be
A kind of heavenly destiny"

and, even the back-and-forth of it, a divine thing.

This knowledge is too wonderful for me; I cannot keep fast hold of it; yet to know occasionally that you are greater than your rhetoric, or your acres of stones, or your woods of worms, worms that may destroy your trees though you spray, is to steady and establish your soul, and vastly to comfort it!

To be greater than your possessions, than your accomplishments, than your desires—greater than you know, than anybody at home knows or will admit! So great that you can leave your plough in the furrow, that you can leave the committees to meet, and the trees to fall, and the sun to hurry on, while you take your seat upon a stump, assured from many a dismaying observation that the trees will fall anyhow, that the sun will hasten on its course, and that the committees, even the committees, will meet and do business whether you attend or not!

This is bed-rock fact, the broad and solid bottom for a cheerful philosophy. To know that they can get on without you (more knowledge than many ever attain!) is the beginning of wisdom; and to learn that you can get on without them—at the close of the day, and out here on your hill in Hingham—this is the end of understanding.

❧❧❧

A people without history is like the wind on the buffalo grass.

—*Sioux saying*

❧❧❧

Sell a country! Why not sell the air, the clouds and the great sea, as well as the earth? Did not the Great Spirit make them all for the use of his children?

—*Speech to President William Henry Harrison at the Council at Vincennes in Indiana Tecumseh (1768–1813), Chief of the Shawnees*

❧❧❧

A little rebellion now and then is a good thing.

—*from a letter to James Madison, January 30, 1787 Thomas Jefferson*

❧❧❧

From

GEORGIA O'KEEFFE

Lloyd Goodrich and Doris Bry

Georgia O'Keeffe was a twentieth-century muralist and landscape painter. Here she talks about how she sees nature.

Nobody sees a flower—really—it is so small—we haven't time—and to see takes time like to have a friend takes time. If I could paint the flower exactly as I see it no one would see what I see because I would paint it small like the flower is small. So I said to myself—I'll paint what I see—what the flower is to me but I'll paint it big and they will be surprised into taking time to look at it—I will make even busy New Yorkers take time to see what I see of flowers. . . . Well, I made you take time to look at what I saw and when you took time to really notice my flower you hung all your own associations with flowers on my flower and you write about my flower as if I think and see what you think and see of the flower—and I don't.

❧❧❧

In these woods reveries sometimes fall upon me so black that I come out of them as if I had had a touch of fever.

—*from* Letters of Madame de Sévigné to her Daughter and Friends
Marie de Sévigné

❧❧❧

There are some who can live without wild things, and some who cannot.

—*from* A Sand County Almanac
Aldo Leopold

❧❧❧

From

THE QUEEN OF THE AIR
BEING A STUDY OF THE GREEK MYTHS OF CLOUD AND STORM

John Ruskin

John Ruskin (1819–1900) was an English critic and writer.

This first day of May, 1869, I am writing where my work was begun thirty-five years ago,—within sight of the snows of the higher Alps. In that half of the permitted life of man, I have seen strange evil brought upon every scene that I best loved, or tried to make beloved by others. The light which once flushed those pale summits with its rose at dawn, and purple at sunset, is now umbered and faint; the air which once inlaid the clefts of all their golden crags with azure, is now defiled with languid coils of smoke, belched from worse than volcanic fires; their very glacier waves are ebbing, and their snows fading, as if Hell had breathed on them; the waters that once sank at their feet into crystalline rest, are now dimmed and foul, from deep to deep, and shore to shore. These are no careless words— they are accurately—horribly—true. I know what the Swiss lakes were; no pool of Alpine fountain at its source was clearer. This morning, on the Lake of Geneva, at half a mile from the beach, I could scarcely see my oar-blade a fathom deep.

What is it that makes it so hard sometimes to determine whither we will walk? I believe that there is a subtle magnetism in Nature, which, if we unconsciously yield to it, will direct us aright. It is not indifferent to us which way we walk. There is a right way;

but we are very liable from heedlessness and stupidity to take the wrong one. We would fain take that walk, never yet taken by us through this actual world, which is perfectly symbolic of the path which we love to travel in the interior and ideal world; and sometimes, no doubt, we find it difficult to choose our direction, because it does not yet exist distinctly to our idea.

—from "Walking"
Henry David Thoreau

༅༄༅༄

From

A SAND COUNTY ALMANAC AND SKETCHES HERE AND THERE

Aldo Leopold

In human history, we have learned (I hope) that the conqueror role is eventually self-defeating. Why? Because it is implicit in such a role that the conqueror knows, *ex cathedra*, just what makes the community clock tick, and just what and who is valuable, and what and who is worthless, in community life. It always turns out that he knows neither, and this is why his conquests eventually defeat themselves.

༅༄༅༄

From

"NATURE"

Ralph Waldo Emerson

Ralph Waldo Emerson (1803–1882), an American poet and essayist, published his first work, "Nature," in 1836.

There are days which occur in this climate, at almost any season of the year, wherein the world reaches its perfection, when the air, the heavenly bodies, and the earth, make a harmony, as if nature would indulge her offspring; when, in these bleak upper sides of the planet, nothing is to desire that we have heard of the happiest latitudes, and we bask in the shining hours of Florida and Cuba; when everything that has life gives signs of satisfaction, and the cattle that lie on the ground seem to have great and tranquil thoughts. These halcyons may be looked for with a little more assurance in that pure October weather, which we distinguish by the name of the Indian Summer. The day, immeasurably long, sleeps over the broad hills and warm wide fields. To have lived through all its sunny hours, seems longevity enough. The solitary places do not seem quite lonely. At the gates of the forest, the surprised man of the world is forced to leave his city estimates of great and small, wise and foolish. The knapsack of custom falls off his back with the first step he makes into these precincts. Here is sanctity which shames our religions, and reality which discredits our heroes. Here we find nature to be the circumstance which dwarfs every other circumstance, and judges like a god all men that come to her. We have crept out of our close and crowded houses into the night and morning, and we see what majestic beauties daily wrap us in their bosom. How willingly we would escape the barriers which render them comparatively impotent, escape the sophistication and second thought, and suffer nature to entrance us. The tempered light of the woods is like a perpetual morning, and is stimulating and heroic. The anciently reported spells of these places creep on us. The stems of pines, hemlocks, and oaks, almost gleam like iron on the excited eye. The incommunicable trees begin to persuade us to live with them, and quit our life of solemn trifles. Here no history, or church, or state, is interpolated on the divine sky and the immortal year. How easily we might walk onward into the opening landscape, absorbed by new pictures, and by thoughts fast succeeding each other, until by degrees the recollection of home was crowded out of the mind, all memory obliterated by the tyranny of the present, and we were led in triumph by nature.

These enchantments are medicinal, they sober and heal us. These are plain pleasures, kindly and native to us. We come to our own, and make friends with matter, which the ambitious chatter of the schools would persuade us to despise. We never can part with it; the mind loves its old home; as water to our thirst, so is the rock, the ground, to our eyes, and hands, and feet. It is firm water; it is cold flame: what health, what affinity! Ever an old friend, ever like a dear friend and brother, when we chat affectedly with strangers, comes in this honest face, and takes a grave liberty with us, and shames us out of our nonsense. Cities give not the human senses room enough. We go out daily and nightly to feed the eyes on the horizon, and require so much scope, just as we need water for our bath. There are all degrees of natural influence, from these quarantine powers of nature, up to her dearest and gravest ministrations to the imagination and the soul. There is the bucket of cold water from the spring, the wood-fire to which the chilled traveller rushes for safety,—and there is the sublime moral of autumn and of noon. We nestle in nature, and draw our living as parasites from her roots and grains, and we receive glances from the heavenly bodies, which call us to solitude, and foretell the remotest future. The blue zenith is the point in which romance and reality meet. I think, if we should be rapt away into all that we dream of heaven, and should converse with Gabriel and Uriel, the upper sky would be all that would remain of our furniture.

It seems as if the day was not wholly profane, in which we have given heed to some natural object. The fall of snowflakes in a still air, preserving to each crystal its perfect form; the blowing of sleet over a wide sheet of water, and over plains, the waving rye-field, the mimic waving of acres of houstonia, whose innumerable florets whiten and ripple before the eye; the reflections of trees and flowers in glassy lakes; the musical steaming odorous south wind, which converts all trees to wind-harps; the crackling and spurting of hemlock in the flames; or of pine logs, which yield glory to the walls and faces in the sitting-room,—these are the music and pictures of the most ancient religion. My house stands in low land, with limited outlook, and on the skirt of the village. But I go with my friend to the shore of our little river, and with one stroke of the paddle, I leave the village politics and personalities behind, and pass into a delicate realm of sunset and moonlight, too bright almost for spotted man to enter without novitiate and probation. We penetrate bodily this incredible beauty: we dip our hands in this painted element: our eyes are bathed in these lights and forms. A holiday, a villeggiatura, a royal revel, the proudest, most heart-rejoicing festival that valor and beauty, power and taste, ever decked and enjoyed, establishes itself on the instant. These sunset clouds, these delicately emerging stars, with their private and ineffable glances, signify it and proffer it. I am taught the poorness of our invention, the ugliness of towns and palaces. Art and luxury have early learned that they must work as enhancement and sequel to this original beauty. I am over instructed for my return. Henceforth I shall be hard to please. I cannot go back to toys. I am grown expensive and sophisticated. I can no longer live without elegance: but a countryman shall be my master of revels. He who knows the most, he who knows what sweets and virtues are in the ground, the waters, the plants, the heavens, and how to come at these enchantments, is the rich and royal man. . . .

In every landscape, the point of astonishment is the meeting of the sky and the earth, and that is seen from the first hillock as well as from the top of the Alleghanies. The stars at night stoop down over the brownest, homliest common, with all the spiritual magnificence which they shed on the Campagna, or on the marble deserts of Egypt. The uprolled clouds and the colors of morning and evening, will transfigure maples and alders. The difference between landscape and landscape is small, but there is great difference in the beholders. There is nothing so wonderful in any particular landscape, as the necessity of being beautiful under which every landscape lies. Nature cannot be surprised in undress. Beauty breaks in everywhere.

❧❧❧

CAMPFIRE ENTERTAINMENT

THE CREMATION OF SAM MCGEE

Robert Service

Robert Service (1874–1958) was a British writer and poet whose poems captured gold-rush life in the Yukon.

There are strange things done in the midnight sun
*   By the men who moil for gold;*
The Arctic trails have their secret tales
*   That would make your blood run cold,*
The Northern Lights have seen queer sights,
*   But the queerest they ever did see*
Was that night on the marge of Lake Lebarge
*   I cremated Sam McGee.*

Now Sam McGee was from Tennessee, where the cotton blooms and blows.
Why he left his home in the South to roam 'round the Pole, God only knows.

He was always cold, but the land of gold seemed to hold
  him like a spell;
Though he'd often say in his homely way that "he'd
  sooner live in hell."

On a Christmas Day we were mushing our way over
  the Dawson trail.
Talk of your cold! through the parka's fold it stabbed
  like a driven nail.
If our eyes we'd close, then the lashes froze till some-
  times we couldn't see;
It wasn't much fun, but the only one to whimper was
  Sam McGee.

And that very night, as we lay packed tight in our
  robes beneath the snow,
And the dogs were fed, and the stars o'erhead were
  dancing heel and toe,
He turned to me, and "Cap," says he, "I'll cash in this
  trip, I guess;
And if I do, I'm asking that you won't refuse my last
  request."

Well, he seemed so low that I couldn't say no; then he
  says with a sort of moan:
"It's the cursèd cold, and it's got right hold till I'm
  chilled clean through to the bone.
Yet 'tain't being dead—it's my awful dread of the icy
  grave that pains;
So I want you to swear that, foul or fair, you'll cremate my last remains."

A pal's last need is a thing to heed, so I swore I would
  not fail;
And we started on at the streak of dawn; but God! he
  looked ghostly pale.

He crouched on the sleigh, and he raved all day of his
    home in Tennessee;
And before nightfall a corpse was all that was left of
    Sam McGee.

There wasn't a breath in that land of death, and I hur-
    ried horror-driven,
With a corpse half hid that I couldn't get rid, because
    of a promise given;
It was lashed to the sleigh, and it seemed to say: "You
    may tax your brawn and brains,
But you promised true, and it's up to you to cremate
    those last remains."

Now a promise made is a debt unpaid, and the trail
    has its own stern code.
In the days to come, though my lips were dumb, in my
    heart how I cursed that load.
In the long, long night, by the lone firelight, while the
    huskies, round in a ring,
Howled out their woes to the homeless snows—O God!
    how I loathed the thing.

And every day that quiet clay seemed to heavy and
    heavier grow;
And on I went, though the dogs were spent and the
    grub was getting low;
The trail was bad, and I felt half mad, but I swore I
    would not give in;
And I'd often sing to the hateful thing, and it
    hearkened with a grin.

Till I came to the marge of Lake Lebarge, and a
    derelict there lay;
It was jammed in the ice, but I saw in a trice it was
    called the "Alice May."

And I looked at it, and I thought a bit, and I looked at
 my frozen chum;
Then "Here," said I, with a sudden cry, "is my cre-ma-
 tor-eum."

Some planks I tore from the cabin floor, and I lit the
 boiler fire;
Some coal I found that was lying around, and I
 heaped the fuel higher;
The flames just soared, and the furnace roared—such
 a blaze you seldom see;
And I burrowed a hole in the glowing coal, and I
 stuffed in Sam McGee.

Then I made a hike, for I didn't like to hear him sizzle
 so;
And the heavens scowled, and the huskies howled, and
 the wind began to blow.
It was icy cold, but the hot sweat rolled down my
 cheeks, and I don't know why;
And the greasy smoke in an inky cloak went streaking
 down the sky.

I do not know how long in the snow I wrestled with
 grisly fear;
But the stars came out and they danced about ere
 again I ventured near;
I was sick with dread, but I bravely said: "I'll just take
 a peep inside.
I guess he's cooked, and it's time I looked"; . . . then
 the door I opened wide.

And there sat Sam, looking cool and calm, in the heart
 of the furnace roar;
And he wore a smile you could see a mile, and he said:
 "Please close that door.

It's fine in here, but I greatly fear you'll let in the cold
    and storm—
Since I left Plumtree, down in Tennessee, it's the first
    time I've been warm."

    There are strange things done in the midnight sun
        By the men who moil for gold;
    The Arctic trails have their secret tales
        That would make your blood run cold;
    The Northern Lights have seen queer sights,
        But the queerest they ever did see
    Was that night on the marge of Lake Lebarge
        I cremated Sam McGee.

THE SHOOTING
OF DAN MCGREW

Robert Service

A bunch of the boys were whooping it up in the
    Malamute saloon;

The kid that handles the music-box was hitting a jag-
    time tune;
Back of the bar, in a solo game, sat Dangerous Dan
    McGrew,
And watching his luck was his light-o'-love, the lady
    that's known as Lou.

When out of the night, which was fifty below, and into
    the din and the glare,
There stumbled a miner fresh from the creeks, dog-
    dirty, and loaded for bear.
He looked like a man with a foot in the grave and
    scarcely the strength of a louse,
Yet he tilted a poke of dust on the bar, and he called
    for drinks for the house.
There was none could place the stranger's face,
    though we searched ourselves for a clue;
But we drank his health, and the last to drink was
    Dangerous Dan McGrew.

There's men that somehow just grip your eyes, and
    hold them hard like a spell;
And such was he, and he looked to me like a man who
    had lived in hell;
With a face most hair, and the dreary stare of a dog
    whose day is done,
As he watered the green stuff in his glass, and the
    drops fell one by one.
Then I got to figgering who he was, and wondering
    what he'd do,
And I turned my head—and there watching him was
    the lady that's known as Lou.

His eyes went rubbering around the room, and he
    seemed in a kind of daze,
Till at last that old piano fell in the way of his wan-
    dering gaze.

The rag-time kid was having a drink; there was no
　　　one else on the stool,
So the stranger stumbles across the room, and flops
　　　down there like a fool.
In a buckskin shirt that was glazed with dirt he sat,
　　　and I saw him sway;
Then he clutched the keys with his talon hands—my
　　　God! but that man could play.

Were you ever out in the Great Alone, when the moon
　　　was awful clear,
And the icy mountains hemmed you in with a silence
　　　you most could *hear*;
With only the howl of a timber wolf, and you camped
　　　there in the cold,
A half-dead thing in a stark, dead world, clean mad
　　　for the muck called gold;
While high overhead, green, yellow and red; the North
　　　Lights swept in bars?—
Then you've a hunch what the music meant . . .
　　　hunger and night and the stars.

And hunger not of the belly kind, that's banished with
　　　bacon and beans,
But the gnawing hunger of lonely men for a home and
　　　all that it means;
For a fireside far from the cares that are, four walls
　　　and a roof above;
But oh! so cramful of cosy joy, and crowned with a
　　　woman's love—
A woman dearer than all the world, and true as
　　　Heaven is true—
(God! how ghastly she looks through her rouge,—the
　　　lady that's known as Lou.)

Then on a sudden the music changed, so soft that you
　　　scarce could hear;

But you felt that your life had been looted clean of all
    that it once held dear;
That someone had stolen the woman you loved; that
    her love was a devil's lie;
That your guts were gone, and the best for you was to
    crawl away and die.
'Twas the crowning cry of a heart's despair, and it
    thrilled you through and through—
"I guess I'll make it a spread misere," said Dangerous
    Dan McGrew.

The music almost died away . . . then it burst like a
    pent-up flood;
And it seemed to say, "Repay, repay," and my eyes
    were blind with blood.
The thought came back of an ancient wrong, and it
    stung like a frozen lash,
And the lust awoke to kill, to kill . . . then the music
    stopped with a crash,
And the stranger turned, and his eyes they burned in
    a most peculiar way;
In a buckskin shirt that was glazed with dirt he sat,
    and I saw him sway;
Then his lips went in in a kind of grin, and he spoke,
    and his voice was calm,
And "Boys," says he, "you don't know me, and none of
    you care a damn;
But I want to state, and my words are straight, and
    I'll bet my poke they're true,
That one of you is a hound of hell . . . and that one is
    Dan McGrew."

Then I ducked my head, and the lights went out, and
    two guns blazed in the dark,
And a woman screamed, and the lights went up, and
    two men lay stiff and stark.
Pitched on his head, and pumped full of lead, was
    Dangerous Dan McGrew,

While the man from the creeks lay clutched to the
  breast of the lady that's known as Lou.
These are the simple facts of the case, and I guess I
  ought to know.
They say that the stranger was crazed with "hooch,"
  and I'm not denying it's so.
I'm not so wise as the lawyer guys, but strictly
  between us two—
The woman that kissed him and—pinched his poke—
  was the lady that's known as Lou.

THE DEVIL IN TEXAS

Anonymous

He scattered tarantulas over the roads,
Put thorns on the cactus, and horns on the toads,
He sprinkled the sands with millions of ants
So the man who sits down must wear soles on his
  pants.
He lengthened the horns of the Texas steer,
And added an inch to the jack rabbit's ear;
He put mouths full of teeth in all of the lakes,
And under the rocks he put rattlesnakes.

He hung thorns and brambles on all of the trees,
He mixed up the dust with jiggers and fleas;
The rattlesnake bites you, the scorpion stings,
The mosquito delights you by buzzing his wings.
The heat in the summer's a hundred and ten,
Too hot for the Devil and too hot for men;
And all who remain in that climate soon bear
Cuts, bites, and stings, from their feet to their hair.

He quickened the buck of the bronco steed,
And poisoned the feet of the centipede;
The wild boar roams in the black chaparral;

It's a hell of a place that we've got for a hell.
He planted red pepper beside every brook;
The Mexicans use them in all that they cook.
Just dine with a Mexican, then you will shout,
'I've hell on the inside as well as the out!'

ULYSSES

Alfred, Lord Tennyson

*Alfred, Lord Tennyson, the British
poet, lived from 1809–1892.*

It little profits that, an idle king,
By this still hearth, among these barren crags,
Matched with an agéd wife, I mete and dole
Unequal laws unto a savage race
That hoard, and sleep, and feed, and know not me.
I cannot rest from travel—I will drink
Life to the lees. All times I have enjoyed
Greatly, have suffered greatly, both with those
That loved me, and alone; on shore, and when
Through scudding drifts the rainy Hyades
Vexed the dim sea. I am become a name;
For always roaming with a hungry heart
Much have I seen and known; cities of men
And manners, climates, councils, governments,
Myself not least, but honored of them all;
And drunk delight of battle with my peers,
Far on the ringing plains of windy Troy.
I am a part of all that I have met;
Yet all experience is an arch wherethrough
Gleams that untraveled world, whose margin fades
For ever and for ever when I move.
How dull it is to pause, to make an end,
To rust unburnished, not to shine in use!
As though to breathe were life! Life piled on life

Were all too little, and of one to me
Little remains: but every hour is saved
From that eternal silence, something more,
A bringer of new things; and vile it were
For some three suns to store and hoard myself,
And this grey spirit yearning in desire
To follow knowledge like a sinking star,
Beyond the utmost bound of human thought.

This is my son, mine own Telemachus,
To whom I leave the scepter and the isle—
Well-loved of me, discerning to fulfill
This labor, by slow prudence to make mild
A rugged people, and through soft degrees
Subdue them to the useful and the good.
Most blameless is he, centered in the sphere
Of common duties, decent not to fail
In offices of tenderness, and pay
Meet adoration to my household gods,
When I am gone. He works his work, I mine.

There lies the port; the vessel puffs her sail;
There gloom the dark broad seas. My mariners,
Souls that have toiled, and wrought, and thought with
      me—
That ever with a frolic welcome took
The thunder and the sunshine, and opposed
Free hearts, free foreheads—you and I are old;
Old age hath yet his honor and his toil.
Death closes all; but something ere the end,
Some work of noble note, may yet be done,
Not unbecoming men that strove with gods.
The lights begin to twinkle from the rocks;
The long day wanes; the slow moon climbs; the deep
Moans round with many voices. Come, my friends,
'Tis not too late to seek a newer world.
Push off, and sitting well in order smite
The sounding furrows; for my purpose holds

To sail beyond the sunset and the baths
Of all the western stars, until I die.
It may be that the gulfs will wash us down;
It may be that we shall touch the Happy Isles,
And see the great Achilles, whom we knew.
Though much is taken, much abides; and though
We are not now that strength which in old days
Moved earth and heaven, that which we are, we are:
One equal temper of heroic hearts,
Made weak by time and fate, but strong in will
To strive, to seek, to find, and not to yield.

❧❧❧

From

MOUNTAINS OF CALIFORNIA

John Muir

There is always something deeply exciting, not only in the sounds of winds in the woods, which exert more or less influence over every mind, but in their varied water-like flow as manifested by the movements of the trees, especially those of the conifers. By no other trees are they rendered so extensively and impressively visible, not even by the lordly tropic Palms or tree-ferns responsive to the gentlest breeze. The waving of a forest of the giant Sequoias is indescribably impressive and sublime, but the Pines seem to me the best interpreters of winds. They are mighty waving goldenrods, ever in tune, singing and writing wind-music all their long century lives. Little, however, of this noble tree-waving and tree-music will you see or hear in the strictly alpine portion of the forests. The burly Juniper, whose girth sometimes more than equals its height, is about as rigid as the rocks on which it grows. The slender lash-like sprays of the Dwarf Pine stream out in wavering ripples, but the tallest and slenderest are far too unyielding to wave even in the heaviest gales. They only shake in quick, short vibrations. The Hemlock Spruce, however, and the Mountain Pine, and some of the tallest thickets of the Two-leaved species bow in storms with considerable scope and gracefulness. But it is only in the lower and middle zones that the meeting of winds and woods is to be seen in all its grandeur.

One of the most beautiful and exhilarating storms I ever enjoyed in the Sierra occurred in December, 1874, when I happened to be exploring one of the tributary valleys of the Yuba River. The sky and the ground and the trees had been thoroughly rain-washed and were dry again. The day was intensely pure, one of those incomparable bits of California winter, warm and balmy and full of white sparkling sunshine, redolent of all the purest influences of the spring, and at the same time enlivened with one of the most bracing wind-storms conceivable. Instead of camping out, as I usually do, I then chanced to be stopping at the house of a friend. But when the storm began to sound, I lost no time in pushing out into the woods to enjoy it. For on such occasions Nature has always something rare to show us, and the danger to life and limb is hardly greater than one would experience crouching deprecatingly beneath a roof.

It was still early morning when I found myself fairly adrift. Delicious sunshine came pouring over the hills, lighting the tops of the Pines, and setting free a stream of summery fragrance that contrasted strangely with the wild tones of the storm. The air was mottled with pine-tassels and bright green plumes, that went flashing past in the sunlight like birds pursued. But there was not the slightest dustiness, nothing less pure than leaves, and ripe pollen, and flecks of withered bracken and moss. I heard trees falling for hours at the rate of one every two or three minutes;

some uprooted, partly on account of the loose, water-soaked conditions of the ground; others broken straight across, where some weakness caused by fire had determined the spot. The gestures of the various trees made a delightful study. Young Sugar Pines, light and feathery as squirrel-tails, were bowing almost to the ground; while the old patriarchs, whose massive boles had been tried in a hundred storms, waved solemnly above them, their long, arching branches streaming fluently on the gale, and every needle thrilling and ringing and shedding off keen lances of light like a diamond. The Douglas Spruces, with long sprays drawn out in level tresses, and needles massed in a gray, shimmering glow, presented a most striking appearance as they stood in bold relief along the hilltops. The Madroños in the dells, with their red bark and large glossy leaves tilted every way, reflected the sunshine in throbbing spangles like those one so often sees on the rippled surface of a glacier lake. But the Silver Pines were now the most impressively beautiful of all. Colossal spires 200 feet in height waved like supple goldenrods chanting and bowing low as if in worship, while the whole mass of their long, tremulous foliage was kindled into one continuous blaze of white sun-fire. The force of the gale was such that the most steadfast monarch of them all rocked down to its roots with a motion plainly perceptible when one leaned against it. Nature was holding high festival, and every fiber of the most rigid giants thrilled with glad excitement.

I drifted on through the midst of this passionate music and motion, across many a glen, from ridge to ridge; often halting in the lee of a rock for shelter, or to gaze and listen. Even when the grand anthem had swelled to its highest pitch, I could distinctly hear the varying tones of individual trees—Spruce, and Fir, and Pine, and leafless Oak—and even the infinitely gentle rustle of the withered grasses at my feet. Each was expressing itself in its own way—singing its own song, and making its own peculiar gestures—manifesting a richness of variety to be found in no other forest I have yet seen. The coniferous woods of Canada, and the Carolinas, and Florida, are made up of trees that resemble one another about as nearly as blades of grass, and grow close together in much the same way. Coniferous trees, in general, seldom possess individual character, such as is manifest among Oaks and Elms. But the California forests are made up of a greater number of distinct species than any other in the world. And in them we find, not only a marked differentiation into special groups, but also a marked individuality in almost every tree, giving rise to storm effects indescribably glorious.

Toward midday, after a long, tingling scramble through copses of hazel and ceanothus, I gained the summit of the highest ridge in the neighborhood; and then it occurred to me that it would be a fine thing to climb one of the trees to obtain a wider outlook and get my ear close to the Aeolian music of its topmost needles. But under the circumstances the choice of a tree was a serious matter. One whose instep was not very strong seemed in danger of being blown down, or of being struck by others in case they should fall; another was branchless to a considerable height above the ground, and at the same time too large to be grasped with arms and legs in climbing; while others were not favorably situated for clear views. After cautiously casting about, I made a choice of the tallest of a group of Douglas Spruces that were growing close together like a tuft of grass, no one of which seemed likely to fall unless all the rest fell with it. Though comparatively young, they were about 100 feet high, and their lithe, brushy tops were rocking and swirling in wild ecstasy. Being accustomed to climb trees in making botanical studies, I experienced no difficulty in reaching the top of this one, and never before did I enjoy so noble an exhilaration of motion. The slender tops fairly flapped and swished in the passionate torrent, bending and swirling backward and forward, round and round, tracing indescribable combinations of vertical and horizontal curves, while I clung with muscles firm braced, like a bobolink on a reed.

In its widest sweeps my tree-top described an arc of from twenty to thirty degrees, but I felt sure of its elastic temper, having seen others of the same species still more severely tried—bent almost to the ground indeed, in heavy snows—without breaking a fiber. I was therefore safe, and free to take the wind into my pulses and enjoy the excited forest from my superb outlook. The view from here must be extremely beautiful in any weather. Now my eye roved over the piny hills and dales as over fields of waving grain, and felt the light running in ripples and broad swelling undulations across the valleys from ridge to ridge, as the shining foliage was stirred by corresponding waves of air. Oftentimes these waves of reflected light would break up suddenly into a kind of beaten foam, and again, after chasing one another in regular order, they would seem to bend forward in concentric curves, and disappear on some hillside, like sea-waves on a shelving shore. The quantity of light reflected from the bent needles was so great as to make whole groves appear as if covered with snow, while the black shadows beneath the trees greatly enhanced the effect of the silvery splendor.

Excepting only the shadows there was nothing somber in all this wild sea of Pines. On the contrary, notwithstanding this was the winter season, the colors were remarkably beautiful. The shafts of the Pine and Libocedrus were brown and purple, and most of the foliage was well tinged with yellow; the laurel groves, with the pale undersides of their leaves turned upward, made masses of gray; and then there was many a dash of chocolate color from clumps of Manzanita, and jet of vivid crimson from the bark of the Madroños, while the ground on the hillsides, appearing here and there through openings between the groves, displayed masses of pale purple and brown.

The sounds of the storm corresponded gloriously with this wild exuberance of light and motion. The profound bass of the naked branches and boles booming like waterfalls; the quick, tense vibrations of the pine-needles, now rising to a shrill, whistling hiss, now falling to a silky murmur; the rustling of laurel groves in the dells, and the keen metallic click of leaf on leaf—all this was heard in easy analysis when the attention was calmly bent.

The varied gestures of the multitude were seen to fine advantage, so that one could recognize the different species at a distance of several miles by this means alone, as well as by their forms and colors, and the way they reflected the light. All seemed strong and comfortable, as if really enjoying the storm, while responding to its most enthusiastic greetings. We hear much nowadays concerning the universal struggle for existence, but no struggle in the common meaning of the word was manifest here; no recognition of danger by any tree; no deprecation; but rather an invincible gladness as remote from exultation as from fear.

I kept my lofty perch for hours, frequently closing my eyes to enjoy the music by itself, or to feast quietly on the delicious fragrance that was streaming past. The fragrance of the woods was less marked than that produced during warm rain, when so many balsamic buds and leaves are steeped like tea; but, from the chafing of resiny branches against each other, and the incessant attrition of myriads of needles, the gale was spiced to a very tonic degree. And besides the fragrance from these local sources there were traces of scents brought from afar. For this wind came first from the sea, rubbing against its fresh, briny waves, then distilled through the Redwoods, threading rich ferny gulches, and spreading itself in broad undulating currents over many a flower-enameled ridge of the coast mountains, then across the golden plains, up the purple foot-hills, and into these piny woods with the varied incense gathered by the way.

Winds are advertisements of all they touch, however much or little we may be able to read them; telling their wanderings even by their scents alone. Mariners detect the flowery perfume of land-winds far at sea, and sea-winds carry the fragrance of dulse and tangle far inland, where it is quickly recognized, though mingled with the scents of a thousand land-flowers. As an illustration of this, I may tell here that I breathed sea-air on the Firth of Forth, in Scotland, while a boy; then was taken to Wisconsin, where I remained nineteen years; then, without in all this time having breathed one breath of the sea, I walked quietly, alone, from the middle of the Mississippi Valley to the Gulf of Mexico, on a botanical excursion, and while in Florida, far from the coast, my attention wholly bent on the splendid tropical vegetation about me, I suddenly recognized a sea-breeze, as it came sifting through the Palmettos and blooming vine-tangles, which at once awakened and set free a thousand dormant associations, and made me a boy again in Scotland, as if all the intervening years had been annihilated.

Most people like to look at mountain rivers and bear them in mind; but few care to look at the winds, though far more beautiful and sublime, and though they become at times about as visible as flowing water. When the north winds in winter are making upward sweeps over the curving summits of the High Sierra, the fact is sometimes published with flying snow-banners a mile long. Those portions of the winds thus embodied can scarce be wholly invisible, even to the darkest imagination. And when we look around over an agitated forest, we may see something of the wind that stirs it, by its effects upon the trees. Yonder it descends in a rush of water-like ripples, and sweeps over the bending Pines from hill to hill. Nearer, we see detached plumes and leaves, now speeding by on level currents, now whirling in eddies, or, escaping over the edges of the whirls, soaring aloft on grand, upswelling domes of air, or tossing on flame-like crests. Smooth, deep currents, cascades, falls, and swirling eddies, sing around every tree and leaf, and over all the varied topography of the region with telling changes of form, like mountain rivers conforming to the features of their channels.

After tracing the Sierra streams from their fountains to the plains, marking where they bloom white in falls, glide in crystal plumes, surge gray and foam-filled in boulder-choked gorges, and slip through the woods in long, tranquil reaches—after thus learning their language and forms in detail, we may at length hear them chanting all together in one grand anthem, and comprehend them all in clear inner vision, covering the range like lace. But even this spectacle is far less sublime and not a whit more substantial than what we may behold of these storm-streams of air in the mountain woods.

We all travel the milky way together, trees and men; but it never occurred to me until this storm-day, while swinging in the wind, that trees are travelers, in the ordinary sense. They make many journeys, not extensive ones, it is true; but our own little journeys, away and back again, are only little more than tree-wavings—many of them not so much.

When the storm began to abate, I dismounted and

sauntered down through the calming woods. The storm-tones died away, and, turning toward the east, I beheld the countless hosts of the forests hushed and tranquil, towering above one another on the slopes of the hills like a devout audience. The setting sun filled them with amber light, and seemed to say, while they listened, "My peace I give unto you."

As I gazed on the impressive scene, all the so-called ruin of the storm was forgotten, and never before did these noble woods appear so fresh, so joyous, so immortal.

INDEX OF AUTHORS

BIBLIOGRAPHY

Abbey, Edward. *Desert Solitaire: A Season in the Wilderness*. New York: Ballantine Books, 1968.

Arnold, Mary Ellicott, and Mabel Reed. *In the Land of the Grasshopper Song: Two Women in the Klamath River Indian Country in 1908–09*. Lincoln, NE: University of Nebraska Press, 1957.

Austin, Mary. *The Land of Little Rain*. 1903, 1931. Reprint. *The Land of Little Rain*. Boston: Houghton Mifflin Company, 1950.

Baker, Russell, ed. *The Norton Book of Light Verse*. New York: W. W. Norton, 1986.

Baron, Robert C., and Elizabeth Darby Junkin, eds. *Of Discovery and Destiny: An Anthology of American Writers and the American Land*. Golden, CO: Fulcrum, Inc., 1986.

Bartlett, John. *Familiar Quotations*. 15th ed. Edited by Emily Morison Beck. Boston: Little, Brown and Company, 1980.

Bartram, William. *The Travels of William Bartram*. Macy-Masius, 1928.

Benson, Adolph B., ed. *Peter Kalm's Travels in North America: The English Version of 1770*. New York: Dover Publications, 1987.

Bird, Isabella L. *A Lady's Life in the Rocky Mountains*. Norman, OK: University of Oklahoma Press, 1960.

Borland, Hal. *High, Wide and Lonesome*. New York: J.B. Lippincott Company, 1956.

Burroughs, John. *Accepting the Universe*. Boston: Houghton Mifflin, 1920. Reprint. *The Complete Writings of John Burroughs*, Vol. 21. New York: Wm. H. Wise & Co., 1924.

Burroughs. *Signs and Seasons*. 1886. Reprint. *John Burroughs' America: Selections from the Writings of the Hudson River Naturalist*. New York: Devin-Adair Company, 1967.

Burroughs. *Leaf and Tendril*. 1908. Reprint. *John Burroughs' America: Selections from the Writings of the Hudson River Naturalist*. New York: Devin-Adair Company, 1967.

Burroughs. *Winter Sunshine.* 1875.

Byron, George Gordon. *Byron: Poetical Works.* Edited by
    Frederick Page. New York: Oxford University Press,
    1970.

Catherine II of Russia. *Correspondance avec le Baron F. M.
    Grimm,* 1878.

Catherwood, Mary. "Marianson" in *Mackinac and Lake
    Stories,* 1899.

Conrad, Joseph. *Nigger of the Narcissus.* New York:
    Doubleday & Company, Inc., 1959.

Davidson, James West and John Rugge. *The Complete
    Wilderness Paddler.* New York: Vintage Books, 1983.

de Sévigné, Marie. *Letters of Madame de Sévigné to Her
    Daughter and Friends,* 1811.

Dickinson, Emily. *The Complete Poems of Emily Dickinson.*
    Edited by Thomas H. Johnson. Boston: Little, Brown
    and Company, 1960.

Edgeworth, Maria. *Ennui,* 1804.

Emerson, Ralph Waldo. "Nature." Reprint. *Emerson's
    Works*, Vol 3. New York: Three Sirens Press.

Frost, Robert. *Robert Frost: Poetry and Prose.* Edited by
    Edward Connery Lathem and Lawrance Thompson.
    New York: Holt, Rinehart and Winston, 1972.

Goodrich, Lloyd and Doris Bry. *Georgia O'Keeffe.* New York:
    Praeger, 1970.

Hay, John. *In Defense of Nature.* Boston: Little, Brown and
    Company, 1969.

Hillerman, Tony. *The Dark Wind.* New York: Harper &
    Row, Publishers, 1982.

Irving, Washington. *The Complete Works of Washington
    Irving.* Edited by Charles Neider. Garden City, NY:
    Doubleday & Company, Inc., 1975.

Jerome, Jerome K. *Three Men in a Boat.* Dent, 1889.
    Reprint. New York: Penguin Books, 1959.

John, Betty. *Libby: The Alaskan Diaries and Letters of
    Libby Beaman, 1879–1880.* Boston: Houghton Mifflin
    Company, 1987.

Knowles, Isobel. "Two Girls in a Canoe." *Cosmopolitan
    Magazine*, October 1905. Reprint. *On the River: A
    Variety of Canoe & Small Boat Voyages.* Edited by

Walter Magnes Teller. Dobbs Ferry, NY: Sheridan House, 1988.

Leopold, Aldo. *A Sand County Almanac: And Sketches Here and There.* New York: Oxford University Press, Inc., 1949.

Lovett, Richard A. *Freewheelin': A Solo Journey Across America.* Camden, ME: Ragged Mountain Press, 1992.

Lewis, Meriwether, and William Clark. *The Journals of Lewis and Clark.* Edited by Bernard DeVoto. Boston: Houghton Mifflin Company, 1953.

Melville, Herman. *Moby Dick.* New York: Random House, 1930.

Merrick, Elliott. *Northern Nurse.* New York: Charles Scribner's Sons, 1942. Reprint. Vermont: Sherry Urie, 1982.

Muir, John. *My First Summer in the Sierra.* Boston: Houghton Mifflin Company, 1916.

Muir. *The Mountains of California.* 1894. Reprint. *The Wilderness World of John Muir.* Boston: Houghton Mifflin Company, 1916.

Nessmuk (George W. Sears). *Woodcraft and Camping.* New York: Dover Publications, Inc., 1963. Originally *Woodcraft.* New York: Forest and Stream Publishing Company, 1920.

Ogburn, Charlton, Jr. *The Winter Beach.* New York: William Morrow and Company, Inc., 1966.

Olson, Sigurd F. *Listening Point.* New York: Alfred A. Knopf, 1990.

Olson. *Reflections From the North Country.* New York: Alfred A. Knopf, 1992.

O'Reilly, John Boyle. *Ethics of Boxing and Manly Sport.* Boston: Ticknor & Fields. Reprint. Originally *Athletics and Manly Sport.* Boston: Pilot Publishing Company, 1890. Reprinted in *On the River: A Variety of Canoe & Small Boat Voyages.* Edited by Walter Magnes Teller. Dobbs Ferry, NY: Sheridan House, 1988.

The Oxford Dictionary of Quotations. 2nd ed. London: Oxford University Press, 1953.

The Oxford Dictionary of Quotations. 3rd ed. London: Oxford University Press, 1986.

Partnow, Elaine, ed. *The Quotable Woman: From Eve to 1799*. New York: Facts On File Publications, Inc., 1985.

Partnow. *The Quotable Woman: 1800–1981*. New York: Facts On File Publications, Inc., 1982.

Patterson, R. M. *Dangerous River*. Don Mills Ontario: Stoddart Publishing Co. Limited, 1989. Reprint. Post Mills, VT: Chelsea Green Publishing Company, 1990.

Powell, John Wesley. *The Exploration of the Colorado River and Its Canyons*. New York: Dover Publications, Inc., 1961. Originally titled *Canyons of the Colorado*. Flood & Vincent, 1895.

Remington, Frederic. "Black Water and Shallows." *Harper's New Monthly Magazine*, August 1893. Reprint. *On the River: A Variety of Canoe & Small Boat Voyages*. Edited by Walter Magnes Teller. Dobbs Ferry, NY: Sheridan House, 1988.

Rich, Louise Dickinson. *My Neck of the Woods*. New York: J. B. Lippincott Company, 1950.

Rinehart, Mary Roberts. *Through Glacier Park*. Boston: Houghton Mifflin Company, 1916.

Roosevelt, Theodore. "Grand Canyon Speech." 1903. Reprint. *Wilderness Writings*. Edited by Paul Schullery. Salt Lake City: Gibbs M. Smith, Inc., 1986.

Ross, Cindy. *A Woman's Journey on the Appalachian Trail*. Harper's Ferry, WV: Appalachian Trail Conference, 1982.

Ruskin, John. *The Queen of the Air: Being a Study of the Greek Myths of Cloud and Storm*. New York: John Wiley & Son, 1869.

Sandburg, Carl. "Prairie Waters by Night," *Cornhuskers*. New York: Henry Holt and Company, 1918. Reprint. *Complete Poems*. Harcourt Brace Javanovich, 1950.

Sandburg. "Buffalo Dusk," *Smoke and Steel*. New York: Harcourt, Brace & World, Inc., 1920. Reprint. *Complete Poems*. Harcourt Brace Javanovich, 1950.

Service, Robert. *The Spell of the Yukon*. New York: Dodd, Mead & Company, 1964.

Seton-Thompson, Grace. *A Woman Tenderfoot*. 1900.

Sharp, Dallas Lore. *The Hills of Hingham*. Boston: Houghton Mifflin Company, 1916.

Stewart, Elinore Pruitt. *Letters of a Woman Homesteader.* Boston: Houghton Mifflin Company, 1982.

Stewart. *Letters on an Elk Hunt by a Woman Homesteader.* Lincoln, NE: University of Nebraska Press, 1979.

Tennyson, Alfred. *The Poetic and Dramatic Works of Alfred Lord Tennyson.* Edited by Horace E. Scudder. Boston: Houghton Mifflin Company, 1898.

Thoreau, Henry David. *The Journal of Henry D. Thoreau.* Edited by Bradford Torrey and Francis H. Allen. Boston: Houghton Mifflin Company, 1906. Reprinted 1949, 14 vols.

Thoreau. *The Maine Woods.* Reprint. New York: Thomas Y. Crowell Company, Inc., 1961.

Thoreau. *Walden.* Reprint. New York: W.W. Norton & Company, 1951.

Thoreau. "Walking." *Atlantic Monthly*, June 1862. Reprint. *The Natural History Essays*, Salt Lake City, UT: Peregrine Smith Books, 1980.

Thwaites, Reuben Gold. *Historic Waterways: Six Hundred Miles of Canoeing Down the Rock, Fox, and Wisconsin Rivers.* Chicago: A. C. McClurg and Company, 1890. Reprint. *On the River: A Variety of Canoe & Small Boat Voyages.* Edited by Walter Magnes Teller.

Townsend, Chris. *Walking the Yukon: A Solo Trek Through the Land of Beyond.* Camden, ME: Ragged Mountain Press, 1993.

Twain, Mark (Samuel Langhorne Clemens). *Life on the Mississippi.* New York: Bantam, 1985.

Van Dyke, Henry. *Little Rivers: A Book of Essays in Profitable Idleness.* New York: Charles Scribner's Sons, 1917.

Wallace, Dillon. *The Lure of the Labrador Wild.* Fleming H. Revell Company, 1905. Reprint. Post Mills, VT: Chelsea Green Publishing Company, 1990.

Whitman, Walt. *The Poetry and Prose of Walt Whitman.* Edited by Louis Untermeyer. New York: Simon and Schuster, 1949.